Smart Kids,
Struggling Readers

Smart Kids, Struggling Readers

The Overlooked Factors and Novel Solutions

Nickie Simonetti

ROWMAN & LITTLEFIELD
Lanham • Boulder • New York • London

Published by Rowman & Littlefield
An imprint of The Rowman & Littlefield Publishing Group, Inc.
4501 Forbes Boulevard, Suite 200, Lanham, Maryland 20706
www.rowman.com

6 Tinworth Street, London SE11 5AL, United Kingdom

British Library Cataloguing in Publication Information Available

Library of Congress Cataloging-in-Publication Data Is Available

ISBN 978-1-4758-4835-9 (cloth: alk. paper)
ISBN 978-1-4758-4836-6 (pbk: alk. paper)
ISBN 978-1-4758-4837-3 (electronic)

∞™ The paper used in this publication meets the minimum requirements of American National Standard for Information Sciences—Permanence of Paper for Printed Library Materials, ANSI/NISO Z39.48–1992.

Printed in the United States of America

After forty years of teaching, where do I begin? To my earliest students (including Mia, Jim, and Jonathan) and those I see today, thank you. Your trust, honesty, and willingness to reveal your truth have taught me well. Your intellectual strength and determination to succeed have been my inspiration.

Also, I thank my eleven-months-older sibling, Theresa. Her handicapping condition provided me with a markedly early exposure to the nature and needs of struggling learners. Hindsight suggests that I have always been a remediation specialist.

Contents

Foreword

We all know the importance of reading. However, I think the person who sums it up best is Dr. Seuss, who wrote, "The more that you read, the more things you will know. The more that you learn, the more places you'll go." *Smart Kids, Struggling Readers* is not just a book to teach children how to read, but rather it is a blueprint for an engine that can take our students to wherever they want to go.

Nickie Simonetti has been teaching children for over forty years and, in that time, she has become a reading teach extraordinaire! However, it is not just the knowledge and skills necessary to teach reading that she possesses. She is insightful, reflective, analytical, and creative and she utilizes all of these qualities to tap into and unlock the potential of her students. Over the years, it has been my privilege to have many earnest conversations with her about the parallel paths of the development of language and reading. We have looked at the trajectories of both, but through the perspectives of our disciplines; mine as a speech language pathologist and hers as a teacher of reading. We have discussed the basics of reading and how intertwined language and reading are, and she has emphasized the importance of the qualitative aspects of teaching reading, such as providing a safe environment where children realize that it is okay to make mistakes, where children feel smart, where children feel successful, and where children take ownership for their learning. Ms. Simonetti has been able to tease out the most effective teaching strategies and develop a pedagogy that results in successful student learning.

This text is a synthesis of her experiences, insights, and creativity; it captures her clarity of vision. It addresses the cognitive, perceptual, linguistic, and affective factors that may interfere with the mastery of reading for students with learning disabilities of any kind as well as with any student who struggles in reading. Her design for teaching will enhance the teaching skills of every teacher and support the students whose lives they touch.

Christine Radziewicz, Doctor of Arts
CCC/Speech Language Pathologist
New York State Teacher of the Speech and Hearing Handicapped
New York State Teacher of the Deaf and Hearing Impaired
New York State School Administrator
Chief Operating Officer, Tiegerman Schools

Note to the Reader

This work is simple and direct. The original techniques and impressions are concise; the presentation and instructional plan no more elaborate than need be. The terms "bright struggling reader" and "Dyslexia" are often used interchangeably. Diagnostic statement is not the point; the behavioral manifestations and corrective process are. The strategies, created for the later, work equally well for both. Furthermore, the methods readily apply to developmental and corrective instruction and expedite adult literacy.

Smart Kids, Struggling Readers is unlike most texts that consider reading instruction. It does not review existing treatment plans, enumerate current approaches, or revisit long-standing instructional practices. It will not regurgitate that which we already know! Instead, this work presents questions seldom asked, interpretations in need of consideration, and factors regularly overlooked. It also introduces *Reading in a Nutshell*, an efficient and effective plan.

Reading in a Nutshell redirects how we view, evaluate, and treat reading failure. The approach, comprehensive yet streamlined, aims to improve prognosis through novel insights and creative strategies. Supplementing the strongest elements of research-based programs, *Reading in a Nutshell* provides crucial components missing from current practice. Through a fast-paced diagnostic-prescriptive model, students come to identify the factors limiting their reading gains.

It is hoped that seasoned educators will find the philosophical and practical insights worthwhile; novice teachers will better understand the issues impacting remedial readers and the dynamics (to encourage and avoid) underlying successful instruction; parents will come to appreciate the complexities surrounding learning to read; and bright struggling students will gain the concepts and strategies to hasten academic growth, renew grit, and restore self-esteem.

Part I

INTRODUCTION

The teacher is no longer merely the-one-who-teaches, but one who is him/herself taught in dialogue with the students, who in turn while being taught also teach. They become jointly responsible for a process in which all grow.

—Paulo Freire

Chapter 1

The Premise

Reading is not hard! Believing in one's ability to read is hard. When students fail in their early attempts at recognizing the printed word, they become trapped in a web of frustration. Moreover, the brighter the learner, the deeper the pit. Resistance due to academic embarrassment, sense-of-self breakdown, and anticipated failure becomes the operational factor. Despite good cognitive ability and ongoing remedial support, prognosis is all too often poor.

We label these students reluctant readers or uncooperative or disinterested or unmotivated or lazy. Unconsciously, we become angered by their failure to thrive. Why? Because in spite of our best efforts and well-honed intervention plans, we barely see improvement. Concurrently, the students recognize our frustration, further reinforcing their sense of hopelessness and deepening their inability to engage.

Rather than underscore academic deficiencies, an efficient plan would capitalize on the students' innate strengths. We know Dyslexic learners come to task with good intellectual potential. *Reading in a Nutshell* takes full advantage of that. Its markedly rapid and positive impact reflects neither wishful thinking nor a magic trick; it is simply a method that brings awareness to bright capable minds.

THEIR PROBLEM

If educators don't succeed, youngsters won't engage; if youngsters won't engage, then educators can't succeed. Teachers struggle when confronted with reluctance and indifference, and students remain reluctant and indifferent when improvement seems nonexistent. We must recognize that student resistance correlates with student frustration, just as learner availability mirrors learner success.

OUR PROBLEM

When bright youngsters struggle with reading, the fault is not theirs. These students require specialized instruction. However, too many higher-level institutions fail to provide teachers with the necessary tools. *Theory (the what to do) is emphasized; practicum (the how to do it) is not.* Also, students are often as impacted by "skill confusion" as they are by "skill deficit." They don't succeed because they don't grasp exactly what is being asked of them. On their own, they cannot interpret the factors that are getting in the way. Our task is to become "translators," clarifying (and so ameliorating) the overt points of interference.

Having taught forty-plus years, I've seen many reading programs come and go. Why are there so many models and so many approaches for teaching a basic skill? Because in spite of their exposure to the newest strategies or continuation in long-standing instructional plans, bright struggling readers continue to struggle. Granted, it may be hard for our students to learn (thus the term "learning disabled"), but it is actually easy for them to be taught. It will be the educator's ability, rather than the student's inability, that will make the difference.

Chapter 2

The Basics

For far too many individuals with average or above intellectual ability, progress under current remedial reading programs is painfully slow. To them, improvement seems nonexistent or unattainable. Skilled educators recognize that these learners have all but given up. They are psychologically bleeding. Our obligation, should we ask them to try again, is to ameliorate the pain swiftly. To accomplish this, an instructional plan must be insightful, effective, and efficient. It must immediately confirm, in the learner's mind's eye, his potential to improve.

We must reestablish in the student a belief that he is indeed bright and capable—not by stating so but by providing experiences that prove it. Given rapid task mastery, the learner will come to see that he can break a long-standing pattern of reading failure. (Reviews of treatment histories confirm years of multiple interventions, multiple techniques, multiple providers, and multiple disappointments.) *The assumption has always been that motivation underlies success; actually, for bright struggling readers, it is success that underlies motivation.*

Reading in a Nutshell proves effective and efficient because the intervention plan rapidly closes gaps, builds skills, and addresses affective needs. This approach recognizes the student's frustration, is respectful of his intellect, and renews grit, the factor most highly associated with academic gains. Furthermore, the original techniques hone error identification (diagnostic monitoring), task awareness (metacognition), intervention options (self-talk), frustration tolerance (defused anxiety), and affective growth (improved sense of self).

WHAT WE KNOW

(1)   Mild reading problems suggest a weakness in a specific processing area.
(2)   More complex reading problems occur when several modalities break down.
(3)   The most severe reading difficulties include a defensive emotional response.
(4)   *Reading failure and future incarceration highly correlate.*

WHAT WE IGNORE

(1)   Bright youngsters initially come to task expecting to succeed.
(2)   Burdensome reading feels joyless.
(3)   Academic failure can manifest in physical symptoms.
(4)   Bright struggling learners develop self-protective mechanisms.
(5)   *Time is not on our side!*

WHY WE FAIL

(1)   Early childhood "wait and see" advice is counter-indicated.
(2)   Most reading programs hone isolated skills.
(3)   Academic struggles (the cause) are attributed to behavioral issues (the effect).
(4)   Technology is meant to supplement, not replace, direct instruction.
(5)   *Research provides a springboard, not a solution.*

HOW THEY RESPOND

(1)   Minimized task engagement (resistance)
(2)   Denied interest (fragile sense of self)
(3)   Rigid and perfectionistic style (fear of failure)
(4)   School avoidance (absence, truancy)

WHAT THEY NEED

(1)   Respect for their ongoing struggle
(2)   Effective, rapidly paced instruction

(3) Continuous Affective Support
(4) Undeniable improvement

WHAT WE NEED

(1) Plans that incorporate our students' good intellectual potential
(2) Approaches that encourage student awareness and self-advocacy
(3) Strong adolescent receptive and expressive language development programs
(4) Peer sensitivity training
(5) Resources that enhance pragmatic skills

Chapter 3

The Given

Reading is basic to academic success. For some the skill comes with ease; for others it is complicated. Bright struggling readers require specific instruction. However, the treatment plan need not be tedious or overly time consuming. Indeed, it should be just the opposite. Also, nothing should be assumed as mastered. For example, a youngster might accurately perform the alphabet song but then ask, "What's an elemenoh?" (the lyric as processed by a child with poor phonemic awareness). Such comments must not be disregarded nor their import minimized.

The Science of Reading considers, evaluates, and confirms the interfering factor. The Art of Reading allows a student to safely approach it. We expedite the learning process by accepting that the latter (the Art) is at least equal to, if not more important than, the former (the Science). We know we cannot teach an unavailable child, and children will remain unavailable when they assume failure. We must recognize that the emotional impacts academic outcome as forcefully as the cognitive. By integrating the Science of Teaching Reading with the Art of Teaching Reading, we support both.

WHAT IS

Current reading programs present some "kernel of truth," some novel insight that expands our knowledge of the reading process. Well-structured and sequentially applied, their strategies address word recognition, or sound blending, or letter-sound association, or linguistic decoding, or contextual analysis, or phonemic awareness. Incorporating confirmed techniques and principles, the methods are described as "evidence-based." Yet, students fail to thrive. Why? Because successful reading instruction requires more than the mastery of isolated technical skills and much more than a rigid compliance to any specific method or approach.

WHAT WAS

An early query assessing the effectiveness of reading methods had been presented by Jeanne Chall in *Learning to Read: The Great Debate*. This work reviewed phonics and whole word instruction. Comparisons were presented; conclusions were drawn. Educators responded by taking sides. This was our initial error! We began to choose, rather than integrate, reading techniques. Even more troubling, we often became rigidly committed to our program of choice, adhering to its prescribed system regardless of outcome.

WHAT SHOULD BE

Successful reading instruction is not the function of an either-or approach. Rather, it is a dynamic, flexible, engaging process. It integrates the best of known strategies into a supportive, interactive, and diagnostic system. Not orderly proceeding from cards one through ten (as too many overly structured programs demand) but rather working with a "shuffled deck." Successful reading instruction is not a rigid, direct roadway to a specific destination. It more resembles a river that ebbs and flows, ever changing (flexible) and ever accommodating (integrating).

Our students will learn how to read words once we learn how to read our students! And this is not hard to do. True, each individual is unique; still most of the perceptual, linguistic, and psychological interferences to reading mastery are not. Overall, the patterns that limit skills development in beginning struggling readers are the same as those that continue to prevent skills development in Dyslexic adults. *Reading in a Nutshell* addresses each. It provides original techniques to effectively and efficiently master, or at least bypass, the factors that are getting in the way.

WHAT TO DO

Reading in a Nutshell hones both the overt and the subtle interferences to academic mastery. It underscores continuous analysis (diagnosis), shared interpretation (informing), rapid intervention (prescription), skills development (ensured accuracy), emotional support (safety), and affective confirmation (student-recognized success). The method examines causative factors and offers appropriate instructional options. And these "options" do not require tedious exercises, continuous flashcard presentations, or endless practice and review. Instead, they reflect spontaneous activities developed from content rapidly presented, queried, and discussed.

The approach ensures a student-teacher team effort where thoughtful analysis replaces repetitive drill. Here, error patterns are interpreted and a range of alternatives (teacher-modeled and student-applied "self-talk") considered. The learner, not solely a recipient, becomes a contributing initiator of instruction. Even the youngest child is a diagnostician, a task analyzer, an overseer. In this way, reading moves from a passive engagement to an active process. The instructor provides insightful discourse and complete academic and emotional support; the student provides trust, grit, and task confirmation.

WHAT TO NOTE

Struggling readers usually experience specific processing difficulties. Most current reading programs will highlight or treat one. *Reading in a Nutshell* moves within and between all contributing factors, prioritizing academic goals while addressing and defusing noted error patterns. The approach aims to concurrently build skills and enhance awareness. Furthermore, the students' affective needs are recognized and supported throughout the remedial process.

For example, should the instructor identify a visual reversal error (b-d substitutions are common in the early stages of reading and writing among Dyslexic and non-Dyslexic students), intervention would address the nature of that miscue. Perhaps the original academic goal had been phonemic analysis. Still, the recognized factor is immediately incorporated into the lesson, even if through no more than a brief aside, "Oh, the letter flipped" (diagnostic impression) and "No big deal!" (Affective Support).

Thus, the original instructional goal is presented as a highly structured, low-frustration, failure-proof task, while the interfering miscue is casually pointed out ("Did you notice . . . ?"). Why? Because, of course, he noticed! We do not want to overload the student; still we cannot leave him in a state of confusion. The teacher must validate the learner's experience and confirm it as a predictable, manageable, and indeed necessary part of the corrective process. In this way, the student comes to see that errors, once a source of embarrassment, are actually "good things," the source of awareness that underlies academic improvement.

Finally, know that for bright struggling readers, engaging in the remedial process often provokes reactions similar to those described in Elisabeth Kübler-Ross's *On Death and Dying*. Be prepared! Our students have been wounded; they will manifest a wide range of emotional responses during reading instruction. Denial, anger, and depression present frequently. We must anticipate their effect on the learning process. Over time, trust and rapport will help ameliorate the impact.

WHAT TO PROVIDE

Active learning, our primary goal for the student, depends on active teaching! We must always be "on," diagnostically and prescriptively engaged throughout the session. Our task is to determine and label the "reading puzzles," those unexplained "dilemmas" that need to be solved. We will continuously experiment with multiple options, ruling out approaches that fail, identifying and incorporating those that do not. Integrating and supplementing the best of known practices provides the pedagogical baseline. Creating original mitigating strategies is the pedagogical challenge! And the more open-minded we are about developing these strategies, the better!

Add to and subtract from your repertoire as need be. Consider student impressions and incorporate their suggestions. For example, to decode multisyllable words, identify and blend the segments from right to left. This technique supports learners who have difficulty holding or recalling (Memory) sound elements (Auditory Association) long enough to combine them into words (Blending).

The Science: Memory holds "last" (the final component) better than "first."

The Art: Decoding may prove more effective if proceeding from right to left.

So, beginning with the last linguistic element, the word "containment" would be decoded as -ment, -tainment, containment. Clearly unconventional, this sequential alternative is not being suggested as a replacement for the more traditional order. Still, it is an option for a "stuck," and that is our task, to provide as many options as possible. By the way, this strategy was created by an adult Dyslexic. Who would know better!

In summary, the current methods for teaching struggling readers leave much to be desired. Too many remedial programs rely heavily on the repetitive drill and practice of isolated skills. True, their academic formats incorporate evidence-based tools. Still, the overall impact is inefficient (years of in-program placement) and ineffective (National Achievement Measures remain of concern). The more successful approach would flexibly integrate a wide range of instructional practices while capitalizing on a bright student's good innate potential.

Finally, remember that we were once grouped into "Whole Word versus Phonics" camps. Now we lean toward "Phonemic Awareness versus Visual Analysis" advocates. Beware of current trends! Research does serve us well. Still, it is only an indicator, not a solution. Its purpose is to provide a source for insight, not groundwork for "pedagogical teams."

Part II

THE METHOD

Education must begin with the solution of the teacher-student contradiction, by reconciling the poles so that both are simultaneously teachers and students.

—Paulo Freire

Chapter 4

Phonics

Some words ("enough," "would") do not follow predictable rules or may be of foreign origin (ballet). They are classified Sight Vocabulary. Some words come close to following predictable rules: they "almost work"; they are "good enough." And some words can be exactly deciphered by applying phonetic or linguistic strategies.

Decoding is a method for combining the isolated sounds of phonetically regular words into meaningful wholes. However, various points of breakdown can interfere with the application of this skill and so undermine a student's attempts at "sounding out" an unfamiliar word. Even more troubling, error patterns (miscues), which should provide the insights to guide a remedial plan, are often overlooked, misinterpreted, or simply found to be baffling.

Letter-to-sound association, Phonics, is among the earliest of academic skills presented to young children. Here, students learn to provide a sound (phoneme) for a given letter (grapheme) and the letter for a given sound. In general, basic songs, games, and practice tasks—all reliant on memory, accurate perception, and concept interpretation—are expected to do the trick. For many, this instructional plan proves effective. However, for some, it becomes the gateway to years of frustration and self-doubt.

FACTOR 1: SOUND AWARENESS

Phoneme manipulation, isolation, and incorporation are prerequisite skills for successful decoding, and Dyslexic students often present as struggling in these areas. However, sometimes a defined "phonemic processing weakness" might be more reflective of a failure to understand the nature of the task at hand. Basically, the learner does not grasp what is being asked of him. Clarification is the key.

For example, rhyming, a basic phonemic awareness skill, is often taught through orally presented word pairs (house-mouse) and lists (cat-hat-mat-bat) or while listening to poems and simple literature. The aim is for the child to recognize an underlying phonetic (sound) match, to understand that words can be organized or manipulated through sound patterns. However, some students fail to identify these relationships. Does this confirm a breakdown in phonological processing? Perhaps not!

Technique

Skills develop quickly when students understand the required underlying concept. We can take advantage of a Dyslexic learner's good intellectual ability to ensure that. For example, rhyming tasks repeating "hat, cat, fat, sat" may do the student no good. However, substituting an exaggerated example (hamburger, samburger, wamburger) will do the trick. Why? The latter more clearly illustrates the task's intent, the specific fundamental notion that the student is expected to grasp.

The instructional principle is simple: ensured concept clarification supports task mastery. When bright students understand what we are asking of them, they will progress. As described previously, a student potentially considered deficient in phonological awareness is now rhyming with ease. Of course, an underlying weakness in auditory sound processing had not been magically corrected. But in this case, the actual difficulty was in the learner's failure to interpret exactly what was being asked of him (the nature of the task). That was the interfering factor, the feature that needed to be addressed.

Therefore, in a nutshell, successful intervention required an accurate diagnosis (we rule out causative factors progressing from gross to subtle) and a modified treatment plan (instruction matched to the suspected need). Had we continued with a more traditional method of repeatedly presenting common rhyming lists ("hat, cat, mat"), we would have only deepened the student's frustration, promoting a pathway to further confusion and its resulting anxiety. We would have actually contributed to a greater problem: Reading Resistance.

FACTOR 2: LETTER-SOUND ASSOCIATION

In the primary grades, students are expected to recite the alphabet and identify its letters. Many can also match the letters to sounds (decoding) and sounds to letters (encoding). However, students who are at risk for reading failure, be they preschool or adult, struggle with establishing these associations.

Reading in a Nutshell provides unique strategies for mastering the required grapheme-phoneme relationships. The techniques directly apply a "known" (the identified letter) to determine an "unknown" (the associated sound).

Although an initial diagnostic screening might reveal inaccurate consonant-to-sound associations, for most reading-delayed students, the greatest struggle lies in retrieving the short vowel sounds. Perhaps they fail to note the subtle nuances that distinguish these closely matched phonemes. In that case, exercises to improve auditory discrimination and/or tasks that apply articulatory feedback may be warranted. However, unless the student specifically struggles with pronouncing short vowels in his oral speech, we can most likely bypass these lengthy treatment plans. For bright struggling readers, the least time-consuming pathway is always the best pathway.

Teaching the Vowels

Letter Form > Visual Mnemonic > Sound

Short vowel mastery as presented in *Reading in a Nutshell* requires a two-part process. The first develops an easily established letter (grapheme) to image (clue) association; the second applies a label (the "word cue" naming that image) to yield the desired sound (phoneme). The approach is simple and clear-cut and always works (Academic Component).

More important, the immediate success with a skill that had been so elusive for so long (the goal: "teach the short vowel sounds" appears year after year on a struggling reader's Individualized Education Program [IEP] or Response to Intervention [RTI] plan) opens a new window of opportunity. Why? Recognizing the ease of mastery, the student wants to come back for more! Trust is established and hope is renewed (Affective Component).

Technique

This vowel letter-to-sound retrieval system differs from current approaches because here the Visual (stimulus) directly yields the Auditory (response). Unlike most Phonics programs that associate a letter name with an unrelated image ("E . . . elephant . . . e"), *Reading in a Nutshell* enhances an image already suggested (partly contained) within the letter form itself. Thus, a portion of the lowercase letter (the "known") transitions into a simple sketch. Then, that image is labeled to establish the verbal cue. Finally, we isolate the initial phoneme in that word cue to yield the desired letter-sound association ("the unknown").

The *Reading in a Nutshell* approach is unique because information, concept, and logic, rather than rote memory or repetitive drill, are the factors underscoring the instructional plan. Indeed, throughout the program, a consistent theme is "You don't need to know it, you only need a way to figure it out!"

STEP ONE

Letter Form > Modification (Clue) > Word (Cue)

Materials: Colored pencils and several flashcards, each displaying a lowercase vowel letter.

Task: The student enhances a feature contained within the letter's form to create an image.

Result: A salient characteristic within the letter's shape is pointed out, modified, discussed, and labeled to yield a "word cue."

The Letter *E*

e > image (a cracked shell) > "egg"

Instruct: While showing a large printed lowercase *e*, use a yellow pencil to draw a zigzag over the horizontal line in that letter's form. State, "This is a crack." Next, draw an egg white and yolk oozing out from the crack. While coloring the yolk yellow, say, "See, this is an egg spilling out from the crack in its shell."

Explain: "When you see the letter *e*, notice the crack (the letter's horizontal line). That's your clue to remember that this letter can make a picture of an egg."

Practice: Provide cards displaying the letter *e* and have the student draw the "clue." He will be making a zigzag over the letter's horizontal line and drawing the "egg" spilling out from that "cracked shell." Concurrently, discussing the drawing, have him describe (verbalize the story association) what he is making.

Question: "What are you making?"

Response: "Egg."

Question: "Egg? How do you know?"

Response: "Because of the crack!"

The Letter *U*

u > image (chevrons attached at the letter's top points) > "up"

Instruct: Show a card displaying a large printed lowercase *u*.

State: "See this letter *u*; it has a line on its left side and another line on its right side." (Trace to darken these noteworthy segments.)

Modify: Use a colored pencil to draw two upturned chevrons (one placed atop the left-side line, the other atop the right-side line). The image now suggests arrows.

Explain: "See, I made two arrows, and these arrows are pointing up. When you see the letter *u*, remember that it can show a picture of arrows pointing up. That is what you should notice; you should think about this picture showing up."

Practice: The child will transition the letter form into the desired image association. Provide several cards displaying the letter *u*, each for the child to modify. He will follow the guidelines demonstrated by the instructor. Also, have the student describe the drawing as he sketches the "clue" (the chevrons) onto the lowercase letter form.

Ask: "What are you making?" Wait for the response, "Up."

Question: "Up? How do you know?"

Response: "Because both sides of the letter point up!"

Confirm: On occasion comment "Good for you!" (Affective Support)

The Letter *A*

a > image (a stem) > "apple"

Instruct: Showing a printed lowercase *a*, use a green pencil to trace over the vertical line on the right side of that letter. Explain, "This is a stem." Draw a small leaf at the base to emphasize the "stem." Next, using a red pencil, trace the circular line of the letter's form and color the interior area red.

Say: "See, this is an apple. When you see the letter *a*, notice the line for a stem. That's your clue to remember this letter can make an apple."

Practice: As before, provide the student with several cards displaying a printed lowercase letter *a* and ask him to draw the "clue" image. Have the student explain his production. Repeat this step several times. Each time, ask, "What are you making?" Wait for and reinforce the reply "Apple."

Question: "Apple? How do you know?"

Response: "Because I see the line that makes a stem!"

The Letter *I*

i > image (man scratching head) > "itch"

Instruct: Showing a printed lowercase *i*, use a pencil to enlarge the dot. Comment, "I am drawing a man. This dot will be his head." Continuing onto the letter's vertical line, draw a stick figure body with arms slanted upward. Then state, "See, this line makes his body." Sketching a hand onto one "arm," comment, "This man has a problem; he has an itch. So, I made a hand for him to scratch it. See, he is scratching his head because that is where he has an itch."

Explain: "When you see the letter *i*, notice the dot to make a head and the line to make the body. Remember this picture shows the man scratching his head because he has an itch."

Practice: Given several cards displaying a lowercase *i*, the child draws the image. Repeating the story association/explanation, he describes the production. Each time, ask, "What are you making?" Reinforce the response, "Itch."

Question: "Itch? How do you know?"

Response: "Because this letter makes a man scratching an itch."

The Letter *O*

o > image (lines extending from the letter's base) > "octopus"

Instruct: Trace over a printed lowercase *o* with a blue pencil, and then draw several short lines extending from the bottom of that letter's circular form. Say, "I am making an octopus. When you see the letter *o*, think of drawing the octopus legs; that's your clue to make an octopus."

Practice: Have the child modify (draw the "clue" image onto the letter *o*) a few cards while repeating the "story" that describes his production. Each time, ask, "What are you making?" As before, reinforce the response, "Octopus."

Question: "Octopus? How do you know?"

Response: "Because I made the legs!"

Practice and Reinforcement

At this point, reinforce the developing Grapheme-to-Image Clue and Image-to-Word Cue Associations. Use sets of student-modified vowel cards and also a group of unmodified cards (an isolated vowel letter without any overlaid image). Present a variety of game-like tasks.

(1) Shuffle all the *child-modified* cards. Have the student sort them into their "story" groups.

(2) Displaying all the *modified cards*, ask the child to pick up only the "octopus" cards, then the "apple" cards, next the "egg" cards, and so on.

(3) Present the *unmodified versions* of the vowel cards (letters without images). Again ask the child to locate the "octopus," "apple," "itch," "up," and "egg" cards.

(4) With each retrieved unmodified card, ask, "How do you know that letter shows octopus (apple, up, etc.)?" The child restates the story association, thus explaining his choice.

(5) Reverse roles. Displaying both image-containing cards and letter cards with no image clue, the child states one of the word cues. The instructor locates the matching cards. Here, occasional teacher "errors" serve

well (confirm student attention, demonstrate frustration tolerance and defused perfectionism, and model grit).

STEP TWO

Word Cue > Sound Isolation > Phoneme Association

Letter (grapheme) to Image (picture clue) Association has been established. We altered each vowel's visual form and provided a story "explanation." We also labeled the image, creating a "word cue." Now, we apply that label. By isolating the word cue's beginning sound, we access the required phoneme (the desired short vowel sound).

Aim

The student will use the initial phoneme in a word cue to yield a short vowel's sound. Success is assured because the teacher remains a diagnostician. For example, a breakdown could occur if the child is unable to identify or isolate a beginning sound in words.

Intervention

This error is auditory in nature. The diagnosis requires a follow-up prescription. (*Reading in a Nutshell* anticipates potential miscues and provides strategies to correct, or at least bypass, any interfering factors.)

(1) The teacher models/instructs by slowly articulating the cue word, pointing to her mouth as the initial vowel sound presents. Next, using slower and more drawn-out speech, pronounces the initial sound (o-) somewhat louder than the remaining word segments (-ctopus).
(2) With each repetition, the initial vowel sound's volume increases, the spacing between sound segments lengthens (o . . . ctopus), and the volume for the remaining segment (-ctopus) decreases.
(3) Gestures can support concept (Sound Isolation). For example, head nodding "yes" while the initial sound is being emphasized and "no" for the word cue's remaining sound segments.
(4) Provide a mirror for the student to watch himself articulate and separate the cue word's segments (visual feedback).

Practice

(1) Pronounce the word cue in a long drawn-out style while emphasizing the initial phoneme ("o"). Then cover your lips (hand placed a few

inches in front of the mouth) and softly state the word cue's remaining sound segments ("-ctopus"). Have the student do the same. Taking turns, loudly articulate the cue's initial sound "o" (auditory feedback emphasized) while decreasing the volume (auditory feedback minimized) and covering the mouth (visual feedback minimized) for the remaining segments, "-ctopus." This "Cover-the-Ending Game" is a lighthearted reinforcer.

(2) Give the child several flashcards, each displaying a visually modified vowel (contains the image clue). Now, articulate a short vowel sound, holding it in a long drawn-out hum. The child will point to the modified card that matches the instructor-provided phoneme "hum." Thus, for example, the instructor "holds" the short sound "o" until the child points to the card displaying the letter *o*. Then, to complete the task, the remaining word segment "-ctopus" is pronounced.

(3) Reversing roles, have the child hum the initial sound as the teacher locates the correlating image-containing letter card. Occasionally (to demonstrate self-monitoring and self-acceptance) make a "mistake" and verbalize the resulting frustration. Provide comments like, "I got that one wrong (self-diagnosis) but it's OK!" (self-acceptance); "I'll try again" (grit).

Mastery

Finally, present cards that show only the letter form (that contain no overlaid image clue). Now, repeating the abovementioned tasks, the student will directly associate letters to sounds (decoding) and sounds to letters (encoding). Goal achieved!

Closure

The academic goals (Sound Isolation and Letter-to-Sound Association) have been met. Next, and of equal importance, we must underscore the student's improved performance. Thus, end the lesson with the comment, "But I thought you didn't know vowel sounds!" This LOL moment is quite valuable. Why? We cannot present a task myriad times with insignificant gains and state, "You're doing fine." *For students to persist, our positive feedback must match their own awareness of skill development.* Improved performance labeled by "the other" (teacher comment) must be validated by "the self" (student-recognized success).

In summary, academic goals are rapidly achieved by progressing hierarchically from a more gross task (teacher developed letter-to-image associations) to finely tuned specific tasks (student generated letter-to-sound retrieval). Concurrently, and equally important, the instructor made frequent errors and owned up to them. Why? We are modeling frustration tolerance, self-awareness, defused perfectionism, and grit (Affective Goals). *Remember, reading struggles impact the whole child; the corrective process must address the whole child.* Failure-proof instruction (academically supported and affectively safe) is the key.

Teaching the Consonants

Letter Name > Articulatory Group > Sound

Most consonant sounds are easily mastered. However, when remedial support is required, intervention moves quickly when logic (remember these are bright students) replaces recall. To achieve this, two basic concepts must be established:

(1)   What a consonant does do
(2)   What a consonant does not do

First, explain that consonants basically lack sound. These letters represent mouth, lip, or tongue placement and not much more. Second, emphasize that "B" is not "buh"; "C" is not "cuh"; "M" is not "muh." Why? The inclusion of a vowel phoneme (the way consonants are usually taught) often underlies future problems with sound blending. For example, a student might read C-A-T, "cuh-a-tuh." Diagnostically, this miscue may not represent a weakness in sound blending but rather might reflect an error in sound insertion (the addition of the vowel phoneme). Ironically, the decoded "cuhatuh" is correct given the data (misinformation) applied.

Technique

Begin with schema/concept/logic. Explain that the twenty-six letters of the alphabet are divided into two groups, consonants and vowels. Next, draw the letter *V*, rotate the image to a horizontal position (<), and sketch "upper lips" onto the top line and "lower lips" onto the bottom. The concurrent discussion includes, "This *V* stands for VOWEL. My adding the lips makes it look like a mouth that is open" (visual image/association explained). Now, correlate this notion with the operational function that "all vowels are letters which open the mouth." Pronounce each short vowel phoneme to demonstrate that action.

The lesson may be further honed by giving the student a mirror to watch himself as he articulates the short vowel sounds. He will notice that his mouth opens while pronouncing each. This quick review of the "known" (the recently taught short vowel sounds) prepares the baseline for "the unknown" (that consonants are the letters that do not open the mouth). This establishes the instructional baseline.

Concept

Naming a consonant letter requires two articulatory motions.

Instruction

The lesson might begin by writing an uppercase *M* and stating its name, "M." Now repeat the letter name "M" several times, each at an increasingly slower rate. Hone the student's attention to the two articulatory movements he can see being produced: an initial motion where the instructor's mouth is open (the projected vowel sound) and a final position when it closed. (He will come to learn that this placement is the desired consonant "sound.")

Continue with this concept. Write the letter *R* and state "R" several times. With each repetition, elongate the pronunciation of that letter's name. Point out that the initial lip position (mouth opened) had changed to a final placement (mouth closed). Supply gestures to provide a visual aide. For example, while stating "Watch R," place the hands alongside your cheeks, the fingers positioned in a puppet-like mode. Slowly articulate the letter name as the fingers expand to correlate with the mouth opening. Then depict the mouth's closing by shutting the fingers. Emphasize, "This closed position is the one that matters, the one that tells R's sound."

Expand the concept. "Now, watch what happens when I say the letter *B*'s name. Again two movements will occur. At first, when saying *B*, my lips are together" (demonstrate and comment, "So you hear nothing"), "and then my mouth opens." Explain, "Now, the eeeee is audible; it is the letter name segment that you can hear." Lastly, have the student place his index finger along his bottom lip and slowly name "B." He should feel (motor feedback) the changes from a closed to an open mouth position. Have him explain what was felt; always confirm concept!

Purpose

(1) The student will note the two articulatory motions produced while naming a consonant letter.
(2) By omitting the vowel phoneme in the consonant's name, he can determine the letter sound.

Theme

"You no longer need to remember consonant sounds; you can just figure them out."

Application

Group I—Here, the projected sound (the vowel phoneme) precedes the noteworthy articulatory placement (the mouth's final position). So, in this group of consonant letters, the desired sound is the lip/tongue/mouth position that remains after saying the letter's name. The consonant letters *M, N, F, L, R, S,* and *X* follow this pattern. They form "The Sound Is at the End" group. (This is the easier group to present when initially developing the skill.)

Group II—Here, the noteworthy lip/mouth/tongue position precedes the projected vowel. This "The Sound Is at the Start" group includes *B, C, D, G, J, K, P, T, V,* and *Z.* As before, demonstrate the articulatory changes that occur while saying these letter names. Make sure the student observes the instructor's mouth movements and any supportive gestures (hand puppet clues). Why? Struggling readers often look away when honing on auditory feedback. True, they will not be able to "hear" a consonant phoneme, but we can still ensure that they "see" it.

To reinforce the developing skill, present the seventeen consonants from Group I and Group II on isolated letter tiles. Sort them into "The Sound Is at the Start" versus "The Sound Is at the End."

Exceptions—In English, there will always be exceptions to the rule. For several consonant letters (*H, W, Y*), the NAMES do not yield the SOUNDS. So, as with the short vowels, use the letter's visual form to create an image clue with a correlating word cue.

Letter	Cue	Mnemonic
H	"hop"	H (Highlight the letter's horizontal line, and provide an image of hopping over a goal post.)
W	"what"	W (Demonstrate a querying motion, and then draw hands at the letter's endpoints and a head onto the center peak. Explain that this image mimics a "questioning" mode.)
Y	"yes"	y (Imitate a neck bending forward to state "yes." Then highlight the slant in y's form to imply that movement.)

Note: Ask the student to create a visually based clue that might work well. Why? A self-determined mnemonic is the strongest mnemonic.

FACTOR 3: THE BABY VERSUS THE BATHWATER

What must our students know and what can they bypass? English has twenty-six letters yet forty-four sounds. Each of these phonemes is represented by an isolated grapheme or a specific letter group (blends, digraphs, diphthongs). Rather than relying on rote auditory memory (most Phonics programs), *Reading in a Nutshell* established twenty-five of these letter-to-sound relationships through Visual Association or Articulatory Logic.

And the rest? Instead of overloading an emerging reader with additional rules, it is more efficient to provide "fill in the gap moments." So, when encountered in print, comment, "Now that's one we didn't talk about . . ." or "You remember that sometimes *g* can make a sound like in the word 'go.'" Then just move on from there! If the student does remember, he has an opportunity to confirm skills development (self-validation). And if not, we provided an emotional safety net.

Through performance monitoring, we will fine-tune the required instructional plan. For example, blends (br, str, fl, gl) will be easily mastered as long as the student avoids vowel sound insertions (decoding st as "suh-tuh"). If st is read as "ts," review left-right scanning. Explain that the visual sequence was transposed ("You flipped") and confirm, "No big deal" (Affective Support). Concurrently, provide assurance that the sounding out and blending attempts were correct, so "Good for you!" Or, perhaps st read "ts" reflected inaccurate sound sequencing. In that case, Lindamood LAC tasks would prove helpful.

Digraphs (consonant combinations like kn and ph) and diphthongs (vowel combinations like au, oi, oo) represent English sounds that can be retrieved through mnemonic or association strategies or identified and reinforced using a reference guide. ("Sound banks" lessen memory load, promote student independence, ensure accuracy, and focus attention on the reading task's main purpose.) Given frequent exposure, retrieval options, and accuracy ensured, these phonetic associations will develop. Moreover, in the interim, the student feels supported and functional.

In summary, unlike Phonics programs that require myriad review and practice exercises, *Reading in a Nutshell* minimizes these tasks. Instead, it hones only those elements our students must know (the short vowel sounds, consonant sounds, accurate blending skills, and digraph and diphthong retrieval options). Aimed at efficiency, it replaces rote memorization with retrieval systems and strategies based on logic, ensured accuracy, and diminished memory load.

Chapter 5

Decoding

Sounding out words is very difficult for struggling readers. Diagnostically, the interfering factors may include problems with associating graphemes (letters) with phonemes (sounds), merging isolated sounds (blending), noting the spatial orientation (reversals and inversions) as well as the order (transposition) of letters in words, maintaining the correct sequence of sounds in words (phonemic processing), and identifying or isolating the sections (syllables) in words. *Reading in a Nutshell* provides methods to correct (original techniques) or bypass (optional strategies) each.

FACTOR 1: LINGUISTIC CLUSTERS

A vowel phoneme (v) plus a consonant phoneme (c) forms a linguistic cluster (vc group). Applying clusters, or rimes, streamlines the decoding process. The Glass Analysis Program identified and categorized these groups years ago. The sequence was based on student-rated difficulty levels. Its booklets, visually clear and well-structured, present each cluster pattern as it expands from a simple trigram (cvc pattern) through multisyllable words. *Reading in a Nutshell* offers an original application to hone cluster identification (visual location), sound association, and auditory closure.

Linguistic Decoding

Visual Association > Sound Association > Blending

Materials

Present a linguistic series (OP- top, stop, stopping) with each word written on a 3 × 6 card.

29

Method

(1)   Exposing the first card, state, "This is OP." (Sound provided; we are teaching not testing!) This is a set (label), a vowel sound, and the consonant sound after it" (definition).

(2)   Provide schema: "Using sets makes reading easier."

(3)   Show the next card (top). Use your left hand to cover the t (op remains exposed). State, "You remember this is op." Note what's happening here; the child is being told, and so accepts, that indeed he remembers. Moreover, since the required response is provided (safety), retrieval errors do not occur (ensured accuracy/supported memory traces). Now, uncovering the t, add "and op changes into . . . " the child reads "top."

(4)   Early Readers: Present the next card (stop). Cover the st and say "op." Expose the t and state, "changes into" the student again reads "top." Exposing the s, "and top changes into . . ." The child reads "stop."

(5)   Advanced Readers: Expanding the series (stop > stoppable > unstoppable), continue to visually isolate the grapheme and morpheme units while providing the necessary sound associations. And so, using both hands, cover all the letters but OP. Review, "You know this is op." Sliding your left hand, reveal *t* and say, "op changes into" the child reads "top." Sliding again, expose *s*. State "and top changes into" the child reads "stop." Next, slide your right hand to cover all segments except *un*. Say, "Remember u + n says un" (accuracy ensured). Then review the full process.

   (a)   Both hands cover all segments except the "set" OP.

   (b)   State, "op changes into" (the left hand exposes *t*), the student replies "top."

   (c)   Continue, "top changed into" (left hand exposes *s*); student response is "stop."

   (d)   "Stop changed into" (expose *un*). The child reads "unstop."

   (e)   Finally, use the left hand to cover "unstop" and expose *able* (the suffix that so far had been covered by the right hand). Ensuring accuracy state, "You know this says –able." Then, revealing each component in isolation, the student will see and then read "op > top > stop > unstop > unstoppable."

So what has been going on here? Letter-to-sound relationships are repeatedly reviewed and practiced, replacing the need for endless flashcard drills. Also, accurate memory traces are assured by providing the required symbol-sound associations. Furthermore, visual processing (tracking and segmenting) is developed. Overall, the technique "trains" visual analysis and supports symbol-sound retrieval, the underlying prerequisites to successful decoding.

Error Analysis

Presented with the word "stop," the student notes OP, adds the *t*, and states "top" and then, expanding to the *s*, reads "sop." Diagnostically, the error might reflect a weakness with noting or blending or incorporating a sound. We immediately address the miscue, momentarily putting aside any planned presentation. The task has now moved from instructional (decoding) to diagnostic (miscue analysis) to corrective (prescription).

Intervention

(1) Define the problem.
(2) Remind the student that he said "sop."
(3) Orally emphasize the sound differences between "sop" and "stop."
(4) Present the card "stop" and repeat the inaccurate response, "sop."
(5) Ask the student to "prove it" ("Show me sop").
(6) Tracking the letters, the reader should notice that the *t* had been omitted.
(7) Confirm, "You figured it out!" (Metacognition). "Good for you" (Affective Support).
(8) Or, should the error continue, WORK IT OUT. Diagnose! Perhaps it was an auditory miscue: sound deletion (sop for stop), inaccurate sound sequencing (tops for stop), or perhaps a visual miscue: grapheme omission (failure to note the letter *t*), inversion (stod for stop), or perhaps something else. Each possibility needs to be considered, and none should be overlooked. (We have all seen educational videos where a student's inaccurate response is dealt with by the instructor looking befuddled yet continuing with the lesson as though nothing had occurred. This stance undermines the reader and is an opportunity lost! We may not immediately "solve a reading dilemma," but we can at least validate that something happened. We owe the student nothing less! Acknowledging the miscue begins the corrective process, an Academic Support. Confirming "We'll figure it out together" provides a safety net, the Affective Support.)

FACTOR 2: SYLLABLE RULES AND PATTERNS

Multisyllable words can make sense! To the struggling reader, they appear intimidating and unmanageable because of their visual complexity. We can defuse this concern by explaining that larger words are made up of smaller basic units (syllables) and that the number of possible patterns (letter arrangements) forming these units is limited. Why? Our students fell less overwhelmed when their options seem finite.

Technique

Cue the learner into the "few" syllable rules, and anticipate potential errors before they occur. For example, in lieu of the traditional format commonly used to represent syllable patterns, substitute a more clarifying version. The following modified format shows long vowel sounds represented by an uppercase V, short vowel sounds indicted with a lowercase v, and silent vowels enclosed in parenthesis. Also, emphasize that every syllable must contain a vowel sound (one vowel phoneme).

Traditional Format		*Modified Format*	
Rule	Sample	Rule	Sample
v	I	V	I
vc	at	vc	at
cv	me	cV	mE
cvc	not	cvc	not
cvce	Home	cVc(e)	hOm(e)
cvvc	coat	cV(v)c	cO(a)t

Instruction proceeds as follows:

(1)   Present a series of single-syllable words (real and nonsense) and have the student match each to its appropriate "rule" or "pattern." This is purely a sorting task. *No reading occurs.* Ask the student to write the uppercase form of those vowel letters whose pattern indicates a long sound.

(2)   Once a student can readily sort isolated syllables into groups and describe a pattern's impact on the vowel sound, join a few of these segments together (pattern combining). This demonstrates the creation of a multisyllable word. Still no reading!

(3)   Explain that syllable patterns represent the "sections" in a word and that each section can be made audible by clapping hands. So, each syllable will yield one handclap (auditory feedback) or finger tap (motor feedback). We can further emphasize the syllable count by writing each of the "sections" on different color index cards (visual feedback).

(4)   Indicate the purpose. "We may not know the word, but we do know how it should sound." For example, if given three syllables (three handclaps and/or index card colors), we know the word might be "elephant" but certainly not "electricity" (demonstrate the five handclaps or finger taps produced when saying that word).

(5)   Now, reading begins. Provide a short list of one-syllable "words" with the "rules" at hand (memory will come with exposure and practice). Have the student decode each. This should be a simple task given the

skills developed so far. However, if the student is unsuccessful, quickly analyze/review/reteach (prescription).

(6) Next, connect two or three of these decoded single-syllable "words" together. The student will read the newly created "multisyllable word."

(7) Larger words (four or more syllables) may require an additional step.

Isolated Syllables > *Syllable Combining* > Syllable Blending

Aim: Reading a larger multisyllable word

Miscue: Failure recalling or sequencing four or more syllables (The Science)

Prescription: Combine segments to minimize the number of units (The Art)

Example: ex + cep + tion + al (isolated syllables = four units)

   excep + tional (syllable combining = two units)

   exceptional (syllable blending = one unit)

FACTOR 3: SYLLABLE IDENTIFICATION

In the abovementioned example, the student is tasked with combining isolated syllables to form a word. He is converting parts into wholes. This is the common classroom practice. But real-world reading requires just the opposite. Students must first determine where a word's syllables are located. *The reader must separate (isolate) the whole (the word) into its parts (the syllables).* For most struggling readers, this is the more difficult task.

Cube Patterns

We can create block patterns (visual arrays) to identify the location of syllables in words. Unique, but not complicated, the color cube arrangements translate standard syllable rules into visual designs. The approach allows the student to "see" the "system at work." Also, the novel presentation promotes on-task behavior and academic independence (Self-Talk: "How would the cube pattern look?").

Materials

(1) Use a small tray divided into four sections.

(2) Color each area (one white, one blue, one yellow, and one "white with a black center dot").

(3) Provide a group of letter tiles, each displaying one grapheme (a vowel or consonant letter), morpheme (prefix or suffix), or common phonetic element (a blend, digraph, diphthong, r-controlled vowel, -le unit).

(4)   Present an array of one-inch cubes (whites, blues, yellows, "whites + black center dot").

Introduction

To begin, we establish the phoneme-to-color associations. Randomly select a few tiles and sort them onto the tray. In the white section, place the single-vowel tiles; in the blue section, the consonant, blends, and digraph tiles; in the yellow section, place the prefix and the suffix tiles; and in the "white + black center dot" section, place the "vowel containing units that yield a consistent sound" (a diphthong, r-controlled vowel, -le unit). Define the unifying features of the groups.

Next, color-match a few of the cubes to the tray. Relate the purpose, "Since the *a* tile had been placed in the white section of the tray, it will be represented by a white cube. The *st* tile (a blend), placed in the blue (consonant phoneme) section of the tray, will be represented by a blue cube. The *au* tile (a diphthong), having been placed in the 'white + black center dot' tray section, will be represented by a 'white + black center dot' cube."

Procedure

Present a phonetically regular trigram (a cvc pattern word). Begin to depict that "word" by noting the vowel. Represent it with a white cube. Next, substitute a blue cube for each of the consonants. Arrange the cubes according to the word's phoneme sequence. This array/pattern now depicts the word. For example, CAT would be represented by a blue cube (the consonant C) connected to a white cube (the vowel A) connected to a blue cube (the consonant T). The array (bwb) becomes a visual depiction of the word (CAT).

Purpose

(1)   We can substitute color cubes for a word's phonemes to create a block pattern.
(2)   Where the array (block pattern) separates into sections, so too will the word divide into syllables.
(3)   Provide and explain the "Segmenting Rules."

The Blue Cube Rules

(a)   Adjacent blue cubes will separate between those cubes.
(b)   A single blue cube most often joins the white cube behind it.
(c)   Sometimes, a single blue cube will join the white cube before it.

The White Cube Rules

(a)   Each white, dotted white, or white "tower" indicates a syllable.

(b)   A single white cube NOT followed by an attaching blue cube is "not trapped" (it is an open syllable). It will yield a long vowel sound.

(c)   A white cube followed by an attaching blue cube is "trapped" (a closed syllable). It will produce a short vowel sound.

(d)   A silent vowel's white cube will "stack" onto a preceding white cube to form a "vowel tower." This pattern indicates a required long vowel sound.

The "White + Black Dot" Rules

(a)   R-Controlled Vowels (ar, er, ir, or, ur)

    (1)   These phonemes are depicted by one "white + black dot" cube.

    (2)   This cube will "seize" (pull over) a preceding blue cube.

    (3)   This cube often ends a syllable.

(b)   Diphthongs (au, aw, oi, oy, oo, ew)

    (1)   Represented by one "white + black center dot" cube.

    (2)   This cube will "seize" (pull over) a preceding blue cube.

(c)   The -le pattern

    (1)   This unit is depicted by one "white + black center dot" cube.

    (2)   The cube will "seize" (pull over) a preceding blue cube.

    (3)   This cube often ends a syllable.

The Yellow Cube Rules

(a)   Prefix cubes are placed a bit before the block pattern.

(b)   Suffix cubes are placed slightly after the block pattern.

(c)   Suffix cubes will sometimes "seize" a preceding blue cube.

Application

With several cubes at hand, follow along with these examples. The task uniqueness may seem confusing at first, but after a few exposures, the concepts become self-evident.

(1)   The Basic Block Pattern: An Open or Closed Syllable

TRUCK

The phonemes are shown by blue cube (TR), white cube (U), blue cube (CK)

The block series (b + w + b) forms the pattern bwb

Rule: A white cube followed by an attaching blue cube is "trapped" (short sound)

The segment bwb > "truck"

APRON

The cubes are white (A), blue (PR), white (O), blue (N)
The cube series forms the array wbwb
This block pattern shows one blue cube between two white cubes
Rule: A single blue cube most often joins the white cube behind it
The array will separate into the sections w/bwb
The first section, white cube (A), has a long sound (the vowel is "not trapped")
The second section (bwb) indicates the white cube (O) is "trapped" (short sound)
The segments w/bwb > w(A) + bwb(PRON) > "apron"

SEXTET

The cubes are blue (S), white (E), blue (X), blue (T), white (E), blue (T)
This series (b + w + b + b + w + b) forms the array bwbbwb
Notice the two adjacent ("touching") blue cubes
Rule: The pattern separates between touching blue cubes (bwb + bwb)
Both of the isolated segments depict a "trapped" vowel (short sound)
The section bwb (SEX) + the section bwb (TET) > "sextet"

MAGIC

The block series is b (M) + w (A) + b (G) +w (I) + b (C)
The block pattern bwbwb shows one blue cube between two white cubes
Rule: The expected pattern bw +bwb > "mA-gic" (A is not trapped; a long vowel)
Or Rule: One blue cube sometimes remains with the preceding white cube
That pattern bwb + wb (A is trapped; the vowel is short) > "mag-ic"

(2)   The Prefix and Suffix Rule: A yellow cube placed before or after a block array

TRADING

Cubes: blue (TR) + white (A) + blue (D) + yellow (ING)
Rule: Suffix cubes (yellow) sometimes seize a preceding blue cube
The series b + w + b + y > the pattern bwby > the syllables bw/by
White cube (bw) is "not trapped" (a long vowel sound)
The segments show bw (TRA) + by (DING) > "trading"

DELIVER

Yellow cube (the prefix DE) is placed to the left of the block pattern
Yellow cube (the suffix ER) is placed to the right of the block pattern
The remaining segment (LIV) is represented by

(a) two blue cubes (the consonant phonemes L and V)
(b) one white cube (the vowel phoneme I)
(c) the LIV cubes form the array b + w + b > bwb
(d) the white cube is "trapped"; short vowel sound

The array (y/bwb/y) > de + liv + er > "deliver"

ENCODING

Yellow cube (the prefix EN) is placed before the array
Yellow cube (the suffix ING) is placed after the array
Blue cubes (consonant phoneme C and consonant phonemes D)
White cube (the vowel phoneme O)
The cube series (ybwby) separates into y (EN) + bw (CO) + by (DING)
Rule: A suffix often pulls a blue cube to it
The bw segment depicts an open vowel ("not trapped"; a long vowel sound)
The pattern > y + bw + by > en + co + ding > "encoding"

(3) The "Stacked" Rule: A silent vowel's white cube will be placed onto a preceding white cube. The result forms a "tower" (W) and indicates a long vowel sound. (A "Modified Syllable Rules" chart can provide a useful at-hand reference.)

MAKE

Cubes: blue (M) + white (A) + blue (K) + white (E)
The series bwbw > the pattern bWb (the silent E cube "stacks" above A)
The bWb "tower" indicates a required long vowel sound
The final array (bWb) > mAk > "make"

COMMUTE

Cubes: b (C) + w (O) + b (M) + b (M) + w (U) + b (T) + w (E)
The cubes b + w + b + b + w + b + w y > the array bwbbwbw
Rule: Separate between touching blue cubes > bwb/bwbw
The bwb segment depicts a "trapped" vowel (a short vowel sound)
The bwbw section forms a "tower" > bWb (a long vowel sound)
Rule: A silent vowel stacks onto the preceding vowel
The final array (bwb + bWb) > com + mUt > "commute"

REPEAT

RE is a prefix (yellow cube placed to the pattern's left)
The remaining cubes: b (P) + w (E) + w (A) + b (T) > bwwb
Rule: A silent vowel "stacks" onto the preceding vowel (bwwb > bWb)
The stacked pattern (bWb) indicates a long vowel sound
The cube array > y (RE) + bWb (PEAT)
The segments indicate the syllables re + pEt > "repeat"

(4) The "White + Dot" Rules: These cubes represent "consistent sound" vowel units

  (a) R-Controlled Vowels:

    FORREST

    Cubes: blue (F) + "white with black dot" (OR) + blue (R) + white (E) + blue (ST)
    Series: b + "w-dot" + b + w + b
    Rule: A second white cube usually pulls the preceding blue cube
    Pattern: b"w-dot"/bwb
    bwb (REST) depicts a trapped vowel (a short sound)
    The array b"w-dot" (FOR)/bwb (REST) > for + rest > "forrest"

    DEPART

    Cubes: yellow (DE) + blue (P) + "w-dot" (AR) + blue (T)
    Series is y + b + "w-dot" + b
    Rule: A prefix is placed slightly to the left of a block array
    The pattern indicates two sections, y/b"w-dot"b
    The syllables are y (DE)/b"w-dot"b (PART) > de + part > "depart"

  (b) Diphthongs

    TOIL

    Cubes: blue (T) + white dot (OI) + blue (L)
    The cube series is b + "w-dot" + b > the cube pattern b"w-dot"b > "toil"

    SCHOOL

    Cubes: blue (SCH) + "white dot" (OO) + blue (L)
    Pattern: b"w-dot"b > "school"

    AUGUST

    Cubes: "white dot" (AU) + blue (G) + white (U) + blue (ST)

Series: "w-dot" + b + w + b
Rule: The second white cube usually pulls a preceding blue cube
The pattern depicts "w-dot"/bwb > au/gust > "august"

(c)   -LE Units

SAMPLE

Cubes: blue (S) + white (A) + blue (M) + blue (P) +"white- dot" (LE)
Series: b + w + b + b + "w-dot"
Rule: The "w-dot" cube (-LE) will "seize" (pull over) a preceding blue cube
Pattern: bwb/b"w-dot"
Note: bwb section depicts a trapped vowel (a short sound)
The pattern yields the segments sam/ple > "sample"

TABLE

Cubes: blue (T) + white (A) + blue (B) + "w-dot" (LE)
Series: b + w + b + "w-dot"
Rule: The "w-dot" cube will "seize" (pull over) a preceding blue cube
Pattern: bw/b"w-dot"
Note: The bw segment shows the vowel is "not trapped" (requires a long sound)
The pattern yields the segments ta/ble > "table"

RESEMBLE

Cubes: yellow (RE) + blue (S) + white (E) + blue (M) + blue (B) + "w-dot" (LE)
The series is y + b + w + b + b + "w-dot"
Rule: The "w-dot" cube will "seize" (pull over) a preceding blue cube
Pattern: y/bwb/b"w-dot"
Note: The bwb section shows a "trapped" vowel (requires a short sound)
The block array depicts the segments re/sem/ble > "resemble"

(5)   More Complex Words

INCOMPREHENSIBLE

Cubes: y (IN) + b (C) + w (O) + b (M) + b (PR) + w (E) + b (H) + w (E) + b (N) + b (S) + y (IBLE)
Array: ybwbbwbwbby

Rules:

(a)   Prefix moves to the left of the array (IN) > y + bwbbwbwbby
(b)   Array divides between blue cubes > y + bwb + bwbwbby
(c)   Single blue cube (often pulled to following white cube) > y +
       bwb + bw + bwbby
(d)   Suffix often pulls the preceding blue cube > y + bwb + bw +
       bwb + by

Pattern: y (IN) + bwb (COM) + bw (PRE) + bwb (HEN) + by (SIBLE)

Note: Vowels follow the "trapped" and "not trapped" rules

Identified Syllables: in + com + pre + hen + sible

Blend (syllable combining): incom + prehen + sible > "incomprehen-sible"

To summarize, *Reading in a Nutshell* presents unique word analysis tools. It provides creative options for grapheme-phoneme retrieval (image clues and articulatory cues), supportive resources (accuracy ensured, modified rules, sound banks), multimodal presentations, and unique syllable identification options (cube patterns). These techniques prove effective because they hone the skills struggling readers must know. They also prove efficient because they minimize excessive Phonics drills and rules (e.g., "schwa"). Our students have neither the time nor the energy for this!

Chapter 6

Sight Vocabulary

DOLCH LIST > PHONETICALLY IRREGULAR WORDS > EFFICIENCY

The Dolch List and Frye List are staples in the teaching of reading. They contain the high-frequency words that make up the bulk of printed material on a page. Mastery supports both reading fluency and written language (basic spelling). Traditionally, these words are taught through repeated exposure to simple texts and/or rote memory flashcard drills. And indeed some common words ("who," "laugh," "does") do require these methods.

Still, given the *Reading in a Nutshell* skills developed so far, many high-frequency words can be decoded with ease ("yes," "must," "then"). As always, aim for efficiency. Rather than present the standard Dolch and Frye lists for memorization, emphasize only the phonetically irregular words. Delete the rest! By substituting a modified list, we serve our students well. The Science: Visual memory for words is often weak in Dyslexic students. The Art: Reducing the number of items relying on rote recall supports struggling readers.

THE MODIFIED LIST

To expedite mastery and minimize memory load, phonetically regular words have been removed from the traditional Dolch and Frye lists. Only those that remain are to be considered "sight vocabulary instant words," that is, words requiring rote memorization.

Pre-K Sight Words

   away, blue, come, find, here, look, my, one, said, the, to, two, yellow, you

Kindergarten Sight Words

   all, are, do, four, good, have, into, our, there, they, want, was, what

First-Grade Sight Words

   again, any, could, from, give, know, live, of, once, some, thank, think,
   walk, were

Second-Grade Sight Words

   because, been, before, both, buy, call, cold, does, don't, goes, many, off,
   pull, right, their, very, work, would, where, your

Third-Grade Sight Words

   carry, done, eight, full, hold, kind, laugh, light, long, only, shall, today, try,
   warm

Noun Dolch Sight Words

   birthday, bread, brother, chair, day, doll, door, eye, father, floor, goodbye,
   head, heart, money, mother, night, school, shoe, song, watch, water, wind,
   wood

Technique

Dyslexia often presents an error pattern of misperceived form (Discrimination) and order (Transposition) of letters in words. Furthermore, salient characteristics (differentiating features) are disregarded (Omission). The words
"were" and "where," for example, are a close visual match; the one is easily
mistaken for the other.
The Science: Struggling readers frequently substitute visually similar words
(was/saw, play/help).
The Art: Emphasizing the salient characteristics in common words serves
students well.

(1) To promote accurate word-to-name association, enhance visual input.
     Highlight the unique features, the "what is different" in words. For
     example, spell similar words (thank/think, horse/house) to underscore
     their distinct letters (auditory feedback). Trace the outlines of similar
     word pairs (box/boy, laugh/light) to hone letter order and spatial place-
     ment (motor feedback). Color-code distinguishing letters (does-goes) to
     emphasize differences (visual feedback).

(2) We can help support memory by providing practice lists that contain words markedly different in appearance (pull/any/said). And these lists should be individualized to meet each student's needs. For sight words causing particular difficulty, create a personalized word bank. This will encourage independence and self-monitoring.

(3) Have students type, rather than write, practice words. There are several reasons for this. One, the approach enhances attention to letter sequence. Also, removing the grapho-motor component (written response) eases the strain on students who find handwriting difficult.

(4) Present a list of four to six Dolch words with corresponding picture clues. (This remains at hand, serving as a reference guide.) Then, providing a group of letter tiles, name the first word.

    (a) The student is to locate the tiles for that word, sequence the tiles to "assemble" the word, mix together (scramble) the tiles, reassemble the tiles to once again form the word, read the word, and then move it to the side. This multitask activity supports recognition and adds an encoding/spelling component. (The Dolch Word List should always be the primary source for encoding practice. Adult Dyslexics still misspell many of these basic words.)

    (b) Present and name the next word. Again, the student will form it with tiles. Then, as before, he scrambles the tiles, reorders them to restore the word, and reads the word. Finally, placing it below the previously formed "tile word," he begins a "tile word list."

    (c) Next, have the student read (practice and review) both words in that "list" and mix all their tiles together. The instructor names the first word for the student to locate from within the shuffled "tile mix." Then names the second word for the student to locate and recreate. Both restored words are read and returned to the side (the "tile word list").

    (d) This "list" expands as words are individually presented. For each addition, the student repeats all of the prescribed tasks. Since every word is "formed, scrambled, restored, and read" when initially "named," and then is again "scrambled, restored, and read" as a member of the "tile word list," the student is provided with multiple opportunities for practice and review.

DOUBLE DUTY WORDS

Homographs are words that look the same (visually match) yet are read differently. This variance reflects usage, that is, whether the word serves as a noun or a verb. He *wound* the bandage over the *wound* is an example. Other words whose pronunciation will be impacted by syntax and grammar include *produce, present, bass, object, dove, lead, record, permit,* and *export.*

In contrast, homophones look different but are read the same. Like homographs, these words require specific instruction. They are best presented as pairs. Associating each word with a visual image (a picture that represents meaning) helps build recognition and definition. Common pairs include sun/son, eye/I, to/too/two, its/it's, their/there/they're, your/you're.

ORTHOGRAPHY

Some word endings sound alike yet are spelled differently. Their purpose is to provide grammatical information. For example, words ending in -cle are nouns (uncle, bicycle) while those ending in -cal are adjectives (tropical, cyclical); the ending -us (focus) indicates a noun, while -ous (famous) serves as an adjective ending. Recognizing these features can help students make sense of reading and spelling.

CONTENT WORDS

Textbooks contain technical vocabulary, words associated with their specific subject matter. For example, English texts discuss punctuation ("colon, exclamation point") and grammar ("noun, preposition"); math books refer to "charts, graphs, denominator, exponents"; science texts describe "convection, cell, kinetic." Textbooks also present functional vocabulary, words that indicate follow-up tasks ("state, define, explain, describe, locate, compare, contrast"). These words might also be categorized as Sight Vocabulary.

Overall, Sight Vocabulary represents more than a memory-stored basic word bank. It can also include the immediate recognition of and purpose for morphemes, functional vocabulary, homographs, homophones, and specific words impacted by syntax, grammar, or subject matter.

Chapter 7

Contextual Analysis

CONTENT > LINGUISTIC GUESS > WORD IDENTIFICATION

Reading passages requires students to move fluidly between ideas. Ideas, not words! It's the application of these ideas that supports word identification. This is the "what makes sense" option. The skill, contextual analysis, is a most important strategy to develop with struggling readers. It is also one of the hardest!

When an attempt at decoding is "good enough," students should be able to apply context and vocabulary knowledge to close any phonetic gaps, any decoding inconsistencies. However, Dyslexic students often tend to be perfectionistic. They readily become "stuck" and rigid when encountering an unfamiliar word. They perseverate on repetitive, albeit unsuccessful, attempts at "sounding it out." Their need is to KNOW the word; they do not want to GUESS it!

The Stuck: All too often, Dyslexic students insist that each word in their word-by-word reading style be correct. Progress is limited by this desire for 100 percent accuracy. More troubling, too many teachers require the same! We seem to jump on every opportunity to correct a misread word. We actually discourage an active and fluid reading style when we announce each error. *Our overvaluing accuracy limits the development of reading skills rather than promotes it.* Why? We are denying the student an opportunity to consider (Self-Talk) or apply developing alternative strategies (Academic Impact). Furthermore, our "badgering" feels endless (Affective Impact).

Contextual analysis encourages the reader to bypass an unfamiliar word, to "skip it," to recognize that when embedded in content, "sounding out" efforts that come "close enough" are usually "good enough" for word identification.

However, this is a remarkably difficult option for a bright struggling reader to apply. Why? The student's impression is that of being "defeated" (as well as humiliated) by the unknown word. Also, the last thing this learner wants is to face further uncertainty ("moving on" implies the likelihood of "moving towards" the additional "unknowns" that are still lurking ahead).

At such times, it is not uncommon to see a student become inflexible, even enraged. He is overtaken by a personal battle with the word at hand. Instructionally, our task (and our struggle) is to get him to proceed, to "move on," to remain fluid, to attempt something else. Often, the most difficult (and most tearful) lessons are those addressing a student's rejection of "good enough" and his refusal to accept "skip it" as an alternative word identification strategy. Why so much resistance? Because to the learner, "That's cheating; I still don't know the word!"

Technique

Our task is to validate that "Skip It" works; to prove that it is an effective and efficient word recognition option. So, when a student insists on "deciphering" a word, cover it. Then, orally read on. Most likely, by hearing the additional content, he will "get it" (determine the omitted word). Also, the student should see that even if he fails to identify the bypassed word, he will continue to acquire information, to draw meaning from the text. His accurate response to a few follow-up questions will confirm that. "See, you didn't know the word but you still managed to learn a lot" (Academic). "Good for you!" (Affective).

Next, and more important than providing an alternative skill (Academic Component) is the follow-up discussion (Affective Component). We must label "the stuck" and emphasize how unhelpful it was. Concurrently, we highlight that by remaining flexible and applying logic, "good enough" and "skip it" did work. With repeated exposure, the student will come to see that he need not "KNOW" a word but rather only needs a method to "DEAL WITH IT." He will come to incorporate contextual analysis as one more tool in his "bag of tricks."

In summary, myriad factors interact in Dyslexia, complicating word identification and leaving the student confused and frustrated. Anyone who has worked with bright struggling readers knows their look of despair while engaged in seemingly impossible tasks. By combining a wide range of recognized techniques (Phonics, linguistic decoding, Sight Vocabulary, contextual analysis) with creative options (unique letter-to-sound retrieval methods, cube patterns, modified rules, streamlined tasks) and self-monitoring strategies (Metacognitive Awareness, Self-Talk), we can better secure reading mastery.

Chapter 8

Oral Reading

ORAL READING > MISCUE ANALYSIS > INSTRUCTIONAL GOAL

Many students will silently read a text and answer follow-up comprehension questions correctly. This leaves the impression that their reading skills are developing well. However, respected educators like Richard Lavoie (*How Difficult Can this Be? F.A.T. City*) have pointed out the folly in this reasoning. One wonders if the focus on silent reading tasks might actually reflect the educational system's own avoidance strategy: "If we didn't hear a reading error, it didn't occur."

It is only through an overt monitoring system, Oral Reading, that we can determine exactly how a learner engages with text. Unfortunately, this is often a most painful task, exposing and belittling the struggling reader. Why? It is the only reading activity from which he has nowhere to hide. The student's frequent miscues, made audible, underscore his limited skills and highlight his deficiencies. As would be expected, one-on-one this activity proves uncomfortable. In a group, it is beyond stressful.

For many, Oral Reading does hold merit. It is obvious that we can see the joy on the faces of young children when they stand before a group to demonstrate their well-developing reading skills. And we know that successful readers do improve phrasing, tone, and pitch while reading orally. However, struggling readers are far too anxious to participate in or take advantage of such lessons. For them, these skills are better practiced through Language Arts activities like plays, storytelling, and poem recital.

Still, Oral Reading yields a powerful diagnostic tool, Miscue Analysis. Here, identified errors are noted and categorized and instructional needs are confirmed. Effective intervention revolves around these gathered insights.

So, how to proceed? We must always protect the student's emotional integrity. To the student, Oral Reading must feel like walking through a minefield. Our student is all but paralyzed by error anticipation as each articulated word challenges his sense of competence and self-worth.

Respectful of this experience, we must avoid correcting every noted miscue. Why? Nothing humiliates a struggling reader more than our underscoring "yet another mistake." Also, we should redefine "error" as "an interference that distorts the author's intent" rather than "a misread word." Thus, miscues are best weighted by their negative impact on meaning. For example: The boy ran down the *road*, read as, "The boy ran down the *street*" is a substitution error that will not affect meaning as much as The boy ran *down* the road, read as, "The boy ran *up* the road" alters the author's message.

Technique

Although everything is diagnostically relevant, educators must remember that the remedial process is an ongoing one. Remain confident that each identified error pattern will eventually be treated, directly or indirectly, over time. Too much all at once does not help! Indeed, it only serves to deepen a student's impression of incompetence. And so, should the student make four errors while reading a single sentence (not uncommon among struggling readers), only one becomes an instructional goal to be addressed at that moment in time.

Factoring in rapport (basic trust) and the student's level of frustration tolerance, a second might be identified ("Remember how sometimes things flip, that's what happened here.") and possibly even another if stated as an aside (a new concept introduced as "No big deal, we can work on that at some other time."). Such comments enhance a student's basic understanding of the multiple dimensions and complications surrounding "how reading works" while setting the expectation (and providing the assurance) that "all will be fine."

In summary, Oral Reading serves well as a one-on-one diagnostic tool (miscue analysis). It is the primary source for determining instructional needs and monitoring skills application. This should be its only purpose! Struggling students gain little by reading out loud (Academic Component). Furthermore, in a regular classroom setting, they find the task to be all but unbearable (Affective Component). Our students live in a world of anxiety; we need not add to that burden. Remember, *Reading in a Nutshell* seeks to support both academic and affective gains. If employed as a "group practice task," Oral Reading is counter-indicated on both counts.

Chapter 9

Fluency

For students to read with ease, they need ongoing opportunities of reading with ease! Therefore, using Instructional Level materials with struggling readers is unproductive. Why? In their experience, texts other than those at the Independent Level equate to a Frustration Level. Regardless of his ability to decipher the words at hand, a student's pending sense of uncertainty while approaching reading tasks, in and of itself, becomes the greatest interference to mastery.

The Science: Per Maslow, safety long precedes the ability to academically engage.

The Art: Nonstressful experiences with reading promote fluid reading.

Through Independent Level materials, we can provide the resource for and reinforcer of continuous reading gains. It is a student's sense of comfort while engaging with text that will promote risk-taking behavior and that in turn will bring materials once considered "too difficult" within the learner's grasp. To some, this may seem an overly guarded or too slowly paced strategy, and so implies the likelihood of unimpressive gains. Actually, for bright struggling readers, the approach ensures the most rapid skills development.

Technique

We do not help the reading-impaired student by pressing too hard. And teacher, student, and parent preoccupation with "grade-level books" serves no one well! To build a fluid reading style, successful intervention adds the next level of difficulty only after the student is completely at ease with the existing level. Thus, we should aim to provide content that comes as close to 100 percent accuracy as possible. (High interest-low readability materials offer easily managed, yet age-appropriate, texts.)

We know that when initially engaging with books, the normally developing reader will choose familiar "favorite" stories to read and reread many times over. He is seeking an experience that is well within his grasp, and thus pleasant and enjoyable. The struggling reader has yet to approach books in this way. By offering materials that support a sense of safety and competence, we can provide that gift. Conversely, if in the student's mind's eye a book is perceived as "too difficult" (a struggling reader's usual impression of Instructional Level texts), we only promote academic overload, frustration, and resistance. Clearly, there is no need to go there!

In summary, to develop a fluid reading style, "easy" (Independent Level reading material) ensures student comfort and so promotes task engagement and its resulting continuous gains; "hard" (per student perception) yields stagnation. It's as simple as that.

Chapter 10

Comprehension

SCHEMA > ACTIVE QUERY > UNDERSTANDING

With frequent exposure, "easy" (Independent Level materials) progresses toward "hard" (Instructional Level materials) minus the correlating anxiety or resistance. Of course, Frustration Level materials should never be part of the mix. However, in the regular classroom setting, most of the presented books, graphs, charts, and handouts are beyond the struggling reader's skill level. So how is the student to deal with this reality?

Our task is to show the child that even when he "can't read it," he can still "use it." For example, chapter headings and images can suggest tools that will correlate with a presented text. The identified resources might include films, outlines, books on tape, content equivalent low-readability materials, teacher notes, and peer input. By utilizing such supports, the learner gains access to the required information. Still, merely bypassing reading level constraints, in and of itself, does not ensure content interpretation or analysis. Successful reading comprehension requires much more.

So where do things actually stand? Currently, effective strategies for improving reading comprehension barely exist. Why? Because common classroom tasks provide redundant guided practice and not much more. That which is being offered as "comprehension instruction" hones "thought matching" rather than "thought development." For example, students are asked specific questions following the reading of a given passage. The "instruction" presents who, what, when, where queries, or applies Directed Reading Activities, or promotes Survey Methods. However, the techniques enhance neither original thinking nor critical analysis.

Within these formats, the student states (query response) or identifies (multiple-choice, summary outlines) information. He provides the "correct answer." He seemingly "manages" the follow-up tasks well (accuracy per-centage). However, his actual understanding is all too often quite limited. Indeed, this student's ability to analyze content or interpret nuance is mark-edly lacking. And while reading a complex text, he is the first to recognize this. His usual comment is, "I just don't get it!" Unfortunately, this compre-hension breakdown is most impacting in real-world situations when he is expected to deal with functional data (Literacy).

So what is going on here? Given standard instructional formats, bright struggling readers will often respond correctly to follow-up queries (which we then credit as evidence of successful passage comprehension). How? They have learned to apply the thought structuring questions which are being provided for them. The problem is they cannot create these questions on their own. *Students are tasked with responding to queries when what they actually need is the ability to generate them.*

Within the classroom setting, reading tasks and texts provide a framework for identifying meaningful data (highlights, italics, topic headings, guided questions). But real-world reading does not work that way. When left to their own devices, struggling readers are unable to determine what is and is not important, when to read thoroughly, where to skim. They see all input as equivalent, misjudging the value or relevance of the specific information at hand. It's as though they are processing a series of bullet points, data identi-fied as necessary yet remaining disconnected.

Reading is thinking, and we must teach it as such. We know that we internally talk with, about, and to reading material in order to process it. We experience interpretation, acceptance, or disagreement as we proceed. We are aware as this occurs. We are good readers! However, this ongoing conversa-tion, engagement, and analysis are all too often missing among struggling readers. Why? They lock into the world of recognizing words rather than of critiquing them.

A stronger approach for developing comprehension would promote self-generated text monitoring and query. We can model that process by reading passages along with the student while verbalizing the thought-enhancing strategies we apply. We underscore our approach for relating to and decipher-ing text by subvocalizing as we read. In this way, we clarify how to engage with the material: evaluating the thesis, honing the argument, asking ongoing questions, noting inconsistencies, feeling a responsive chuckle, recognizing enlightenment.

Technique

Successful reading comprehension requires active engagement and effec-tive language processing. Rather than solely providing practice with texts or reading passages, we can better promote higher-level comprehension through language puzzles to solve, directions to apply, and quandaries to think through. In this way, we replace structured follow-up questions with open-ended analysis. Self-query ("What must I know and how do I use it?") becomes the key to successful task completion. Now students are moved from a passive engagement (noting content) to a result-oriented process (interpreting and applying the information at hand)

(1) Arithmetic word problems are curt and to the point. Presenting such unembellished text is a strong starting point. Items repeating the same data (yet worded differently) force thoughtful analysis. For example:

Mike has five guppies all the same size. Together he has twenty inches of guppies. How long is each guppy?
Mike has four-inch-long guppies. Altogether, he has twenty inches of guppies. How many guppies are there?
Mike has five guppies. Each is four inches long. How many inches of guppies does he have?

This task is twofold. The obvious component is to determine "an answer." The more important piece is to note how or why the information varied and the effect that had on our thinking it through. It is this second factor that strengthens reading comprehension.

(2) Projects. Step-by-step directions for art or science projects provide excellent opportunities to monitor comprehension. The hands-on engagement supports attention to details. Moreover, the student will note exactly when something starts to go wrong (comprehension breakdown) via immediate feedback (unexpected outcome).

(3) An alternative DRA (Directed Reading Activity) strategy reverses the roles. Have the student choose a text and then create follow-up questions for the instructor to answer. Make "mistakes" so he can explain where your thinking went wrong.

(4) Card games and magic tricks. Read the directions along with the student to determine the rules for play (Academic Component). Then enjoy (Affective Component).

(5) "What Would You Do?" queries. These tasks prove most helpful for building critical thinking. Here, the logic applied to a simple scenario varies based on some minor change in the criteria. For example:

Sue notices someone taking another person's school lunch.

(a) What might she do?
(b) What might she do if it is her best friend taking the lunch?
(c) What might she do if she knows the person taking the lunch is poor and hungry?

(d) What might she do if she dislikes the person whose lunch had been taken?

(e) What might she do if she knows the person already ate lunch and is only trying to be hurtful?

(6) Importantly, this task also supports social comprehension (pragmatic skills), an area in need of development for many of our students. Present "What Would You Do?" tasks with a series of facial expression picture cards and a list of possible replies. The student is to match the facial expression to its correlating response. Also, offer some cards (or emojis) with no response. Have the student decide on the probable comment.

(7) Syntax complicates comprehension. Within similar sentences, the words might match yet the meaning varies. For example, "The boy put the box near the toys" versus "The boy put the toys near the box." Imaging, a visualization technique, is a strategy that clarifies the distinctions.

Demonstrate: Set the schema by arranging each word for both sentences on isolated flashcards. This emphasizes the word consistency yet hones the sequential mismatch.
Task: To emphasize the differences in meaning, introduce "imaging." Have the student "think how the story would look were he watching it on TV." Then ask him to describe (replying to a step-by-step guided query) the scene.

Sentence One: The boy put the box near the toys.

(a) Query: What does the boy look like? How old is he?

Response: Short blond hair, five years old

(b) Query: What color is the box? How big is it?

Response: Black, big, and heavy

(c) Query: What kind of toys? How many?

Response: Three small cars

(d) Query: So, how does this story look? What do you see?

Response: I see a small boy trying to carry a big, heavy box. He takes it next to his toy cars and puts it down.

(e) Comment: Yes, I agree (confirmation) and I bet he is happy to put it down since the large box must have been hard for him to carry (modeling inference).

Sentence Two: The boy put the toys near the box.

(a) Query: What does the boy look like? How old is he?

Response: Short blond hair, five years old
Comment: OK, I see the same boy.

(b) Query: What color is the box? How big is it?

Response: Black, big, and heavy
Comment: OK, I see the same box.

(c) Query: What kind of toys? How many?

Response: Three small cars
Comment: OK, I see the same toys.

(d) Query: So, how does this story look?

Response: I see a small boy carrying three small cars. He brings them next to a big box.

Concept: Noting the similarities and differences in the sentence meanings.

(a) Query: So, did the two stories look the same?

Response: No.

(b) Query: Why not?

Response: For one, the boy had to pick up a heavy box, but for the other he had to pick up three small cars.
    Comment: We also noticed one story had the boy look tired (Inference).
    So the two "TV shows" (images) looked different, and that proves the two sentences do not mean the same thing. They meant different things, even though all the words were exactly the same.

(8) Inferencing: Continue the analysis. Have the student serve as a TV director leading his actors through the scene ("Walk slowly, the box is very heavy. Don't drop it! Wipe the sweat from your face. Look tired."). This strategy hones details (the facts) and considers outcomes (implications).

(9) Vocabulary can be a presenting problem. Our usual concern is "Does the student know what a word means?" However, often it is not the word's meaning as much as its multiple meanings that distort comprehension.

Also, some students may fail to interpret a word in context because they are trying to apply their earliest (chronologically based) word association. For example, a bright high school student may be baffled by a simple sentence like *The woman was about to bare a child.* Why? He is trying to understand how "bear," his initial word association, fits into this story line.

(a) Expose the learner to homophones and multiple-meaning words.

He hit the top of the top top (top = highest point; top = best in class; top = a spinning toy).

(b) Emphasize the impact syntax, grammar, and context (subject matter) have on word meaning (definition vs. intention).

(10) A High-Interest Option: Allow some ten to fifteen minutes a day for "In Class Texting." Cell phones are everywhere, so we may as well take advantage. When students participate in a classroom text conversation, they interpret information, opinion, "slang," and abbreviations. They reply to and engage with the content. They are comprehending!

(11) Modify Standard Practices: Traditional follow-up reading tasks can be altered to better hone comprehension. For example, two-column note-taking strategies (a technique that distinguishes main points from supportive details) are commonplace. Expanding the format to include a third column provides a space for query and commentary. The location might house student-teacher discourse considered and evaluated during class discussion, that is, the higher-level interpretations and implications that go beyond a text's factual data.

(12) *While skilled readers use the presented words (text) to recognize ideas (concepts), struggling readers rely on ideas (concepts) to identify the presented words.* For this reason, pre-establishing schema is crucial. The learner must enter the task with a significant foundation, a baseline, if he is to make effective use of reading material. We must develop the resources that will provide that underlying scaffold:

(a) Prepare the learner before reading takes place. For example, orient your student by establishing the task's purpose (pleasure reading, a follow-up written report) and any relevant background information (e.g., the story's setting vs. real-time setting).

(b) Read aloud the first chapter (Eileen Simpson's *Reversals: A Personal Victory over Dyslexia* points out this import) to familiarize the student with the writer's style (sentence complexity, word choice). *Also, reveal the plot and (when available) watch the movie beforehand.* Our aim is for students to understand literary nuance, the "what makes this a great work." Laboring through the "what is being said" limits a student's attention to the "how was it said" (unique plot or character development, twists and turns, metaphors, referents, etc.). These are the elements that embody literature's deeper purpose.

(c) Teach students how to annotate, produce margin notes, summarize (a few sentences to restate the page content, written in the whitespace below), and "flag" (using different colored Post-its, each associated with a theme, character, conflict, or favorite passage) the text.

In summary, effective reading comprehension relies on effective language processing. Its purpose is practical; its goal is literacy. Instruction requires much more than presenting a series of who, what, when, why questions. Successful reading comprehension is measured in student-generated active query and independent content application. *It is not verified by an acceptable score on some computer-based assessment.*

Chapter 11

Visual Processing

IDENTIFIED FACTOR > AWARENESS > INTERVENTION

With the recent focus on phonemic awareness, the impact of visual attention and visual processing on reading development has been downplayed. Current research leans toward the consensus that the salient issues in Dyslexia reflect problems with phonemic analysis. Some interpretations go so far as to associate poor handwriting with a failure to note sounds in words.

However, researchers (Scarborough, 2005) have questioned the import of phonological awareness as a primary causative factor. They point out that measures considering the impact of letter identification (27 percent of the variance in reading level) outweigh the impact of phonemic awareness (21 percent of the variance in reading level) and that reading failure can be noted among students with no significant impairment in phonemic processing. For them, reading struggles correlate with nonphonological measures.

Researchers like the French linguist Frank Ramus accept that Dyslexia presents issues in visual imagery, visual analysis, and visual gestalt. These processing difficulties underlie errors in the discrimination of details (the orientation of a letter's lines and curves), visual recall (word recognition), and visual-spatial organization (left-right or top-bottom letter placement). Given this wide range of potentially interfering factors, we must be careful not to limit treatment options to any "either-or" scenario (visual analysis vs. phonemic awareness).

Also, be aware that faring well on specific IQ tasks (WICS: Block Design) does not confirm visual processing as an area of strength. That conclusion can misdirect a treatment plan. For example, a perceived "visually strong" youngster might still disregard the orientation, form, placement, or sequence of similar letters (*b-d*) and words (play-help). Perhaps this inconsistency reflects our equating two unequal tasks. One (Block Design) is three-dimensional, manual, engaging, and novel; the other, reading letters and words, is not (two-dimensional, linguistic, frustration filled, and anxiety provoking).

PART ONE: BOOKS

Concepts of Print must be intact. It is not uncommon to see bright, experientially rich youngsters who have little understanding of how books work; who will scan a text from right page to left page; who cannot identify the basic units of structure (a letter, a word, a sentence, a paragraph); who overlook punctuation and capitalization; and who disregard the table of contents, index, and glossary or are unaware of the purpose they serve.

A book's visual presentation supports meaning. The noteworthy features include the pictures, passage headings, and text style (italics, highlights). Educators often presume a student's awareness of this basic knowledge. However, for struggling readers, it requires direct instruction. For example, an older student may need to be taught that the table of contents represents an author's basic outline; that a word followed by a comma, a group of additional words, and then another comma implies vocabulary meaning or referent; and that pictures, sketches, graphs, and charts are visual representations intended to clarify and enrich an adjacent text.

Developing the awareness of and purpose for this highly supportive visual information is a necessary part of the struggling reader's instructional plan. Without it, reading comprehension (and so reading interest) suffers. However, these goals are seldom included in an IEP or RTI (classroom intervention) plan. They should not be overlooked. Nor should many other visually impacting factors like word density, text format, or choice of font be disregarded.

Visual Density

The frequency of reading errors logically correlates with the number of words on a page. However, the nature of this breakdown may be more affective than academic. Why? Word difficulty seems to impact accuracy less than word count (density). For example, students will often read a short sentence containing higher-level complex words with more ease than a longer passage made up of much simpler, even basic, words. It seems the student's impression that a text looks overwhelming makes it overwhelming!

Technique

Page appearance, in and of itself, can limit frustration tolerance and undermine sustained on-task behavior. To minimize such interference, we must monitor and, when need be, modify the visual format of the presented text (the letter size, word spacing, line spacing, font style, sentence length). Even the choice of paper (background color) can prove meaningful. Overall, the intervention plan resembles a visual training process more than an academic skill.

Promoting student comfort with content embedded within dense formats (crowded text, lengthy passages, small type, and minimal white space) requires a hierarchical approach. Initially, present lists of isolated short sentences whose formats are visually clear and uncomplicated. Use a large standard font, and provide ample white space. Maintaining this style, begin to combine several sentences to create short paragraphs. Over time, gradually decrease the letter size and word spacing. Concurrently, increase the number of words and the sentence lengths. Finally, merging isolated paragraphs, create longer passages that transition into high-interest stories.

Be sure the increased difficulty level reflects an expanding visual tolerance and not enhanced word recognition (decoding level). *Dolch Readers* offer chapters composed primarily of basic words, a material in keeping with this desired goal. As skills build, reformat the stories (alternative fonts, decreased type size, minimized white space). Continue this process until the practice texts visually match the reading materials in the student's regular classroom setting.

PART TWO: WORDS

Our student may accurately decode (letters into sounds) and blend (sound combining) orally presented words yet fail to recognize these items when viewed on paper. Perhaps they are reversing (id read ib) or rotating (id read ip) or transposing (id read di) the letters at hand.

Appropriate instruction would explain these miscues, confirming and illustrating the specific points of breakdown. In this way, we can develop the learner's ability to anticipate ("what might go wrong") and so ameliorate ("what will make it right") his unique error patterns.

To begin instruction, present a flashcard displaying the word CAT. Pointing to the letters, state "C-A-T spells CAT, agree?" Then, while writing the word, restate "C," "A" (place the A to the left of the letter C), "T" (place T to the right of the C). Now ask, "This shows the word CAT, agree?" Use this example to explain that a written word must more than contain the required letters, the letters must also appear in the required order. Emphasize, "How it looks matters!"

Visual Discrimination

Visual discrimination is the ability to note the salient characteristics (the similarities and differences) in letters and words. Matching activities comparing shapes, pictures, and colors provide useful introductory tasks to establish a conceptual baseline. However, these exercises should be short-lived. The more effective prescription applies academically relevant tasks, that is, the visual matching of similar letters and words.

Technique

(1) Present tracking exercises for basic words. This supports both visual discrimination and Sight Vocabulary. Two for one whenever we can get it! Materials like *The Michigan Tracking Program* offer well-structured and visually clear practice activities.

    (a) Present a basic sentence followed by a short series of visually similar words.

The boy ran.
A This The Those They bag
boy dot bay run man ran ray

    (b) Read the full sentence once. Then point *to (while restating) the first word. The student locates that word (heard and seen) from within the follow-up array. This is purely a matching task. If correct, move on to the next word (teacher pointed to and read). If not, wait while the student continues to scan. (Comment is unnecessary. Why? We avoid "No" whenever possible. Our students hear that word often enough. In most cases, the wait-time alone will cue the need to search further.)

        *When "pointing" to a word, align your finger to run along, rather than under, the sentence. This continually lessens the exposed visual stimuli, hones word location, and emphasizes left-to-right tracking.

    (c) Present a somewhat expanded version of the original sentence followed by an expanded array of visually similar "words." Repeating the procedure, the student sees and hears the full sentence and then, in isolation, sees, hears, and locates each word.

The big boy ran.
These The Then bid bog did big dig bad
bay boy bag run ray hun man rau ran han

(d)   In total, provide some five or six practice tasks (each a further expansion of the original sentence and of the follow-up array).

(e)   Add an encoding (spelling) component. Present the sentences on cards and dictate each. (Accuracy is ensured because the visual stimulus remains at hand.) Allow the learner to check his work by matching it to the model (Academic Component). Praise his self-monitoring (Affective Component).

(f)   The student sentences are to be written one under the other. This keeps an accurate stimulus within the learner's visual field (ongoing monitoring).

(g)   Lastly, ask him to read the sentences. (Note: If the student's letters are poorly formed or inaccurately placed on the line, word memory can be negatively impacted. Moreover, if he cannot read his own handwriting, the task becomes affectively painful. To avoid these consequences, use the teacher-made copy.)

(2)   Visual Modifications

(a)   Provide supports that enhance visual clarity (enlarged type, Irlen color overlays).

(b)   Build compensatory strategies. For example, to ameliorate b-d confusion, demonstrate that removing the top loop from B ("the known") yields b ("the unknown").

(c)   Use color-coding and "bolding and fading" strategies to hone left-right sequence.

(d)   Our students often have fine-motor issues. They grip a pencil close to its base. A helpful rule is "Stay off the sharpened part." This enhances visual feedback while writing.

(3)   Prove It!

A most effective follow-up strategy for active visual monitoring had been presented in The Reading Recovery Program. Here, the student "proves" his response by tracking each letter in a word. The process confirms that the sound he seeks (the phoneme) is represented by the letter he sees (the grapheme) and that it appears at the expected location.

(4)   Affective Confirmation

This Reading Recovery strategy is a corrective tool used to address miscues (the "what went wrong"). However, the technique is equally valuable to underscore reading gains (the "what is going right"). Our students get ample opportunity to note when they fail. We must highlight when they succeed. Having students "prove" a correct response is empowering (self-validating). Also, asking students to "prove" accurate responses alters their long-standing expectation that teacher input solely addresses "mistakes" (Affective Component).

(5) Figure-Ground Confusion

Sometimes students seem to hone on the ground rather than the figure (e.g., confusing the letters *t* and *w*. Both create the appearance of a triangular white background behind their letter forms.) Instructionally, it is worth discussing the suspected factor. Right or wrong is not the point! We are confirming that something "happened" and that the interpretive process is active and ongoing. In this way, the reader discovers that an error might indeed make sense, that it may be explainable, that considering "What just happened?" is basic to learning.

In summary, inaccurate visual processing impacts reading mastery. Promoting visual attention, expanding task tolerance, and developing error analysis serve our students well.

Chapter 12

Phonemic Processing

IDENTIFIED FACTOR > AWARENESS > INTERVENTION

Rhyming skills and letter-sound association, components of phonemic awareness, had been discussed earlier. Blending, another phonemic processing skill, is the ability to combine isolated sounds or word parts into recognized wholes. It is a prerequisite to accurate phonetic and linguistic decoding. Although readily mastered by most, exercises in sound expansion, sound holding, and articulatory modeling support those who require instruction.

The Lindamood-Bell Program had introduced articulatory feedback as a remedial tool. This strategy, developed through a speech-language model, provides a unique and most helpful "kernel of truth." Emphasizing lip, mouth, and tongue placement, the technique enables a student to "feel" letter sounds. However, some learners may master the skill of matching an articulatory placement with a letter name (LiPS) and may also identify that letter's sound location within a word (LAC-3) yet still have difficulty merging isolated phonemes. For them, transferring "the what is felt" (motor) into "the what is joined" (blended) is a huge leap.

This seems particularly true for blending consonants. Why? To blend the phonemes a + t ("at"), the student moves from an open mouth position (the articulated vowel) to a closed mouth position (the consonant placement), a fluid motor transition. But combining s + t requires a closed mouth to closed mouth movement (i.e., consonant placement to consonant placement), a more difficult articulatory performance. It seems the successful merging (blending) of consonant sounds requires some additional, albeit very subtle, motion, a sort of "tongue glide" (s + t > "st") or "lip pop" (b + r > "br") or "air flow" (f + l > "fl").

Without that transitioning factor, output remains as isolated letters or as letters joined through sound insertions ("bring" blended "boring"). So now what? Our role is to consider the presenting behavior based on observation and student explanation (often described as a "tongue stuck" phenomena) and to explore the probable causative factors and possible intervention tasks. This is the progression that underpins all effective teaching: noted behavior (student impression and performance) to diagnosis (the suspected feature to be ruled out) to prescription (a specific instructional plan).

Technique

To blend isolated consonant sounds, students must recognize the intermediate motion that joins them. This "connector" needs to be identified, to be felt. Why? A student cannot produce "what goes right" until he understands "what has been going wrong." Also important, note his baseline, that is, the ability to articulate a consonant blend. For example, if the word "string" is pronounced "shring," a prerequisite or concurrent intervention plan might include Speech Therapy.

Next, ensure sound awareness. Present a group of words that contain a consonant blend and hone the student's attention on that phoneme's articulatory consistency regardless of its location within a word (initial > *st*all, medial > mi*st*ing, final > lo*st*). Arrange the presentation so that the desired sound is heard in the final position (lo*st*), then the initial position (*st*all), and, lastly, the medial position (mi*st*ing). This sequence supports concept.

Now, slowly pronouncing the consonant blend, use hand signals to demonstrate the motor point of merger. For example, "st": glide your index finger in an upward swing-like motion to mimic the tongue's rising movement as it flows from behind the bottom teeth ("s") to the roof of the mouth ("t"). Work toward noting/highlighting/emphasizing the positional change, the connecting movement (a "tongue rise") that had occurred. Instruction will progress from modeled task to supported practice to student independent application.

In summary, sound blending is a basic phonemic processing skill. However, it can be a difficult one to master, particularly for consonant letter groups (digraphs and trigraphs). Through teacher input (explanation of task requirements, modified presentation, honed point of juncture, supportive visual clues), the student will recognize (awareness) and incorporate (application) the required articulatory movements. This instruction, although unnecessary for most, addresses a "stumbling block" for some. When needed, the intervention proves essential.

Chapter 13

Language Processing

Reading difficulties reflect language difficulties. Successful learners demonstrate accurate phonemic awareness, verbal reception, syntax and grammar, flexible word usage, and comprehension of idioms and common expressions. Weakness in any of these language realms will negatively impact reading development.

In younger children, receptive and expressive language processing difficulties are often recognized. Both parents and teachers will note students who fail to follow oral directions, seem inattentive when listening, or misperceive verbally presented information (Receptive Language). Also noted are those students who cannot relate their thoughts and ideas, who use awkward sentence structure, or whose poor articulation makes their oral expression difficult to understand (Expressive Language). In both these cases, remediation (Speech and Language Therapy) is usually provided.

There are also many older students who do not process language well. However, for them, the discrepancy between intellectual potential and functional language performance is often overlooked. Why? Bright youngsters compensate well! It is not surprising, for example, to find underlying word naming issues (Dysnomia) in a student who presents as having a superior oral vocabulary (he substitutes "crimson" because he cannot retrieve "red").

Also, IQ Verbal Scores used to imply language mastery measure expressive content (knowledge base of response), not expressive usage (syntactic and grammatical quality of response). And, in general, Adolescent Language Screenings do not delve deeply enough to identify subtle expressive or receptive weaknesses. Finally, behavioral manifestations associated with language processing deficits may be misdiagnosed as an attention deficit disorder (ADD).

So, how does an older student with an undiagnosed language processing deficit present? Receptively, he might understand the gist of a class lesson yet will fail to note, prioritize, or incorporate most of the relevant details. Or, just the opposite; he may capture the details but not see the gestalt. Also, he might misinterpret vocabulary (idioms, homonyms), mishear words ("Plato" perceived as "play dough"), overlook alternative definitions (multiple-meaning words), or disregard the impact of syntax and grammar on word and sentence meaning.

Expressively, this student will demonstrate sufficient basic word knowledge, articulation skills, and command of simple sentence patterns to get by. Still, his overall language usage is curt; its content sparse. He is often frustrated, aware of what he wants to say but unable to fully get it out. And he is markedly anxious when expected to speak before a group. Finally, lacking in pragmatic skills, he may be socially awkward or verbally inappropriate.

Technique

To support an older student's receptive skills, fine-tune the role transition words play in merging ideas. Help him determine if they support/enhance (furthermore, also) content or contrast/negate (however, but) information. Also, categorize technical vocabulary according to subject matter. For example, Visual Arts will use the terms "negative space" and "halftone," Theater refers to script and prop, Technology introduces output and binary, Music discusses treble and quartet, and History describes serf and dynasty. In this way, we help organize/cluster concepts.

Confirm that the student understands instruction/direction vocabulary. Though commonly presumed mastered, it often is not. For example, older students who have underlying issues with semantic processing do not realize that the terms "compare and contrast" mean totally different things. Lastly, help the student recognize that subject matter impacts word meaning (*period* as defined in History class vs. English class; *poll* in Gym class vs. Statistics class). Failure to grasp a word's content-specific usage will distort comprehension.

Expressively, the reluctance to participate in classroom discussion is often understood by a teacher and explained by the student as "being shy." Actually, it is the spontaneous nature of oral conversation that hampers the ability to engage. Interestingly, this same youngster may write complex essays and rich stories, expressive language tasks. How? Here, output was no longer time specific. The learner had ample opportunity to consider vocabulary options, enhance/expand sentence structure, or rework theme and organization.

We can promote oral participation by granting that necessary processing time. For example, meet with the student before class to preview a lesson's content and present the planned follow-up questions. This provides him with an opportunity to ponder the data and formulate his response. Also, predetermine which questions he might be asked to address. In this way, we help defuse the student's performance anxiety.

Finally, recognize the uncertainty these older students feel when speaking before a group. We cannot "encourage" that away. Rather, creative options will be required. For example, word comprehension need not be confirmed through a standard dictionary-like definition but instead could be verified via student-provided images, sentences, and stories. During classroom oral presentations or debates, have the student serve as a moderator (query cards in hand) rather than a presenter. This will lessen spontaneous language demands (and its correlating anxiety) while still promoting active class participation.

In summary, language processing deficits in older students do exist! Unfortunately, they are often unrecognized or, even worse, misdiagnosed. Their impact limits social engagement and academic mastery (content comprehension, class participation) and contributes to frustration, anxiety, and poor sense of self.

Chapter 14

Affective Support

PRESUMED FAILURE > ANXIETY > STAGNATION

Few things limit academic progress more than the student's own expectation of continued failure. Existing reading programs overlook the import of this factor. They understand and treat reading difficulties as academic features, disregarding the impact of student emotional frustration and self-disappointment. We must address these concurrently presenting problems if we hope to expedite reading gains.

CONSIDERATIONS

(1) Dyslexia correlates with good intellectual potential. However, bright struggling readers come to doubt their innate ability. *They interpret academic failure as intellectual limitation.* We must make it clear that they are intelligent people who think in unique and interesting ways. Early on, describe (to even the youngest) a general overview of how the brain works and how we learn and integrate information. Honor the student's strong potential by confirming that although he may struggle with "learning it," he is very capable of "understanding it."

(2) Our students must recognize that the skills prerequisite to good reading are manageable and finite. Presenting a modified scope and sequence chart will help clarify, and so demystify, the task requirements.

(3) A defined problem always proves less troubling than an ongoing state of confusion. For the bright struggling learner, diagnosis presents as a relief rather than a concern.

(4) Learning requires an active and flexible thinking style. Academic risk-taking will follow confidence and that will follow success and that will follow effective instruction. We need to present a fail-proof intervention plan to ensure this progression.

(5) Explain that you are "not a tutor" (struggling readers most likely have had plenty of those) but rather someone who will help them know how to use their good thinking and how to apply their capable minds. Ensure them from the start that they will not be going through more of the same, that this work will be something different.

(6) We recognize that struggling readers fail to meet our expectations. We overlook the fact that they fail to meet their own! Very early on, these students know that things are not "OK." They do not understand the why (Dyslexia), but they consistently experience the what (failure to thrive). The result is a diminished sense of self-worth and overwhelming feelings of incompetence.

(7) Be aware that just as Dyslexia is complicated, so too is the job of the learning specialist. Why? *Because academic remediation is a therapeutic process*. This proves to be profoundly true and quite a dilemma. We are teachers, not psychologists. We must tread with great care! Still, our students' emotional reactions to years of failure cannot be ignored. Also, and important to note, a struggling reader's academic frustration cannot be addressed in a psychotherapist's office as efficiently and poignantly as it can be within the remedial setting itself. Why? Here the student can reflect on his emotional pain at the exact moment a miscue inflicts its correlating "ouch."

INTERVENTION

Bright struggling students are trapped in a cycle (fear of failure > resistance; resistance > limited progress; limited progress > sense of hopelessness; hopelessness > refusal to engage; refusal to engage > continued failure). What to do? Discussing concepts like those suggested in Gail Sheehy's work *Passages: Predictable Crises of Adult Life* proves helpful. Her baseline presents the theory that negative experiences at various stages of human development remain alive within us. For our students, it is the internalized frustration of early reading failure that takes on a life of its own.

Behaviorally, it is a very young and wounded child who has the regular "temper tantrums," who is emotionally running away from the reading tasks at hand. If left unresolved, this "force" will continue to negatively impact the learner throughout his academic career. Resistance and indifference are "how it presents." Anxiety is "where it comes from." Rage is "where it is willing to go!" I can recall a graduate professor's explanation "Babies last stand in alphabet land." The interpretation suggested that student resistance reflects a desire to stay in "Babyville," a prereading world.

But why would bright children seek to remain in a place where they present as less able than their peers, where the adults in their world seem confused and disappointed, and where they fail daily? More likely, their behavior was not a choice but rather a response. Even in those earliest of school years, bright struggling learners were already developing avoidance techniques. Over time, the residual memories of confusion and inadequacy became the operational factors. The student was no longer the one in control; he was under the influence of his overwhelmed "younger self."

We have all seen youngsters who refuse to look at a book, or continually glance away from the page, or rock back and forth leaning toward and then away from the reading material at hand. Painful to watch, these students are literally both physically and emotionally swaying in and out of the learning process. What is going on here? An academic task "feels" unmanageable. The student assumes failure. The internalized "little child" runs away from the "intolerable place." Task availability has been undermined by task insecurity.

Techniques

We must explain this dynamic to our students (regardless of their age). The concept is presented as a two-part lesson. The first will confirm, "I cannot teach you what you already know." The goal here is to establish the need for risk taking, a feature that underlies all new learning.

The discussion goes something like "Suppose I tell you I am going to teach you how to spell cat, C-A-T. See, now you can spell cat. But you already knew how to spell cat, so saying I was teaching you that word did nothing to help you learn. Your brain had that information. I did not help you because I can only teach you new stuff, stuff that your brain does not already know. So, you will notice that our work is going to be mostly new stuff. Then I will be teaching you. That's how I can help!"

The second theme explains that there are long-standing feelings from an insecure child that still exist within. The learner must notice when its "power" is interfering with mastery and must know that this "little one" (the previously unsuccessful self) can be controlled. The dialog goes something like "That was an earlier part of you, left over from when you were a younger child, an emerging reader."

Next, clarify the distinction between then and now. "So, although that part of you will always exist, it no longer has power over your learning how to read. The proof is that you will be learning to read! The little child did not learn to read and that's why he hurts so much. But you can learn to read, and that is what matters! Tell that inner child to stop worrying because he will never have to read; you will take over the job. He can relax. You will be the reader."

It is remarkable to see how quickly students connect to this "internal little child" concept and how they respond with interest, relief, and a sense of empowerment. Now, during instruction, when things seem to not be going well and the learner backs away from engagement, point out the situation and state, "Did you feel that? (there is often a physical reaction, an identifiable feeling). That's the little child; that's not you! He worries that he can't do this work, and he is right . . . but remember you can!" At this point, the instruction must be so fully supportive, so guaranteed to work, so perfect in presentation, that the student has no alternative but to succeed.

And that success is the required component; the validation that things are improving. With time, as the student develops a variety of academic options and better understands his specific interferences to learning, he will require less intensive support. He will come to identify the "belly ache" as "the little one getting scared" and recognizes that the experience can be used to his advantage. Now, a once-limiting event becomes a cueing system, indicating that closer attention is needed. "See, your little child is telling you that it's getting harder. He is letting you know it's time for your best work. You will figure it out because you know what to do!"

In summary, our students' affective struggles impact mastery as much as their linguistic and perceptual struggles. It is a reality that must be addressed! We are not therapists, but we are engaged in a therapeutic process. By applying concepts like those presented in the Sheehy scenarios, we can help defuse the residual anxiety connected to early reading failure.

Chapter 15

A Cautionary Tale

Dyslexia is never "cured"; it is managed! Even with marked improvement, our students will require continued classroom supports and modifications. On a positive note, unlike most academic tasks that center around individual production (test taking, report writing), most life tasks do not. In the real world, we work in settings where multiple contributors create a final product (team analysis, group projects). Here, Dyslexics prove rather successful. Why? They have experienced years of negotiating task requirements, seeking additional input, and tolerating frustration. Moreover, they are the creative thinkers, the contributors who work outside the box.

Our mandate is to get them through the academic years feeling whole, competent, and intelligent and to minimize the intensity and duration of their pain along the way. Instructionally, it is not enough that a remedial approach proves effective; it must also be efficient. For the bright struggling reader, one more day in a world of failure is one day too many. If we come to terms with nothing else, we must at least recognize this: *Time is of the essence.*

Part III

THE PRACTICE

Liberating education consists in acts of cognition, not transferals of information.

—Paulo Freire

Chapter 16

Guidelines

In review, the Science of Teaching Reading emphasizes specific research-based techniques known to enhance skills development. Most of today's reading programs apply these strategies, evidence based and statistically validated. Their formats move along point by point, step by step. For the teacher, the prescriptions are logical, sequential, and easy to follow. In contrast, the Art of Teaching Reading is far less predictable. It requires educators remain intuitive and interpretive, a very different skill.

Reading in a Nutshell does not present a specific system. Rather, it requires a multisided continuous integration. It hones methods that identify the interferences to mastery (diagnosis), explain and label error patterns (awareness), and promote highly supportive, rapidly paced, and anxiety-defusing intervention plans (prescription). Developing skills are alluded to, applied, and thrown into the mix as need be. The pot is constantly stirred, cognitively, linguistically, and emotionally. Overall impressions remain of the moment, representing our best guess. As student awareness builds, the learner himself will confirm or rule out the suspected factors:

(1) Remember the "Kernels of Truth," the original techniques contained in remedial reading programs already available to us. Do not discard their creative insights, but be warned not to get bogged down in any overly repetitive or overly structured implementation. Perceive these existing tools as helpful, not as sacred.

(2) Apply strategies and techniques fluidly. Do not diligently move from one level/task/card to the next level/task/card. This is much too time consuming, passive, thought limiting, and redundant! Once the academic point is made, move on! If some practice "packs of cards" remain, so be it!

(3) Be aware of "remedial stucks." Repeating a task many times over with little or no apparent improvement is the clue that something is not working. Efficiency demands that we seek an alternative!

(4) Diagnostic insights identified by the instructor are to be translated for and demonstrated to the student. So, should he read *bad* for *dad*, the error is pointed out and explained ("You flipped; I'll show you.") to hone both awareness and instruction (Academic Component).

(5) Remediation is an exhausting process! We must recognize the ongoing feelings of frustration (theirs and ours) and the seemingly endless required efforts (theirs and ours). Just as we take care of the learner, we must remember to take care of ourselves. Supportive goals are required for both members of the student-teacher team. Occasional reminders of "where things were" compared to "where things are" serve everyone well (Affective Component).

(6) We must not forget our own limitations. In spite of the many "How To" guides we read or the professional development programs we attend, it is foolish to believe that our students will ever "overcome Dyslexia." The disorder's impact is lifelong!

(7) We must accept that Dyslexic students suffer from a chronic condition we will never be able to fully understand. Its effects and manifestations are befuddling. Our most enlightened, honest, and empathetic response simply comes down to, "Boy, isn't that something!"

Chapter 17

Application

The following are samples of *Reading in a Nutshell* in action. The first example presents a general treatment overview (Scope and Sequence). The second offers a more detailed case study, highlighting some of the academic and affective stumbling blocks.

CASE STUDY: A TREATMENT OVERVIEW

Subject:

Middle School Student Diagnosed with Dyslexia
Strengths: Bright and verbal
Weakness: Primary-level reading skills
Affect: Discouraged, overwhelmed, academically depressed

Intervention Plan:
Twice weekly one-on-one lessons (thirty minutes each)

Week One:

Academic: Short vowel presentation and mastery; Trigram decoding and
    encoding
Affective: Student reconnects with his potential for academic success

Week Two:

Academic: (a) Concept: Vowels versus Consonants
            (b) Analysis of visual and phonemic processing errors
Affective: Discussion of the emotional interferences to learning

Week Three:

> Academic: (a) Sorting and decoding (cvc, cVce, cVvc patterns)
>   (b) Present linguistic clusters (two-syllable words)
> Affective: Noting, labeling, and DEFUSING miscues

Week Four:

> Academic: (a) Multisyllable decoding and encoding
>   (b) Oral reading (miscue analysis)
>   (c) Introduce syllable "cube patterns"
> Affective: Self-validation (The student brings a graphic novel to the session. He reports, "I did what you showed me and for the first time I didn't throw the book away.")

Impact:

> Academic: Rapid skills development
> Affective: Student > Academically hopeful
>   Teacher > Delighted for the child!

Summary:

> Rapid academic development occurs when we provide honed instruction and incorporate a struggling learner's good intellectual potential. This treatment plan reflects a team effort. The tasks were diagnostic, hierarchical, interpretive, and integrative. Improvement was teacher labeled (Academic) and student confirmed (Affective).

CASE STUDY: A DETAILED SAMPLE

Subject:

> Student: Bright six-year-old, grade 1. Nonreader
> Referral: Inability to form letter-sound associations
> Affect: Diminished sense of self. Immature style
> Behavior: Low frustration tolerance. Academic avoidance

Motivators:

> Extrinsic rewards
> Strong desire to please parents
> Highly competitive

Format:

> Two 30-minute one-on-one lessons per week
> Duration: Five weeks (ten sessions)

Intervention

Session One

I pick up the student at his classroom door. The child insists his mom does not want him working with me. "Mom says I don't have to do this!" He is argumentative and rigid.

Response: "OK. Come to my office to write Mom a note. That way, she will know we agreed not to work together." He accepts. As we walk toward the workspace, interaction becomes more positive. The student responds to queries about his family and pets. Rapport begins.

In the room, I present paper for the note and then (while cutting the paper into strips) ask if he knows how to make a "Helicopter." Intrigued, he engages in a simple Origami Lesson. We produce several models (this provided an opportunity to assess his language comprehension, attentional style, spatial concepts, fine-motor integration, and memory skills). Next begins a "helicopter flying contest" (of course, he repeatedly wins, promoting a sense of fun, safety, and competence in a remedial setting). The session is over.

Walking back toward his classroom, I express frustration with my poor "flying skills" and with "losing every game" (modeling the emotional response to repeated failure). "Maybe I will win next time" (suggesting things can change and setting an expectation to work again). "I will try very hard to practice" (implying grit and the import of follow-up work). Summarizing the session, "Oh, we forgot to write the note to Mom. She will think I am seeing you again. Should we work together another time?" He agrees to continue with the lessons. The remedial process has begun!

The student recognized:

(1) He need not control the situation.
(2) He is safe. (Basic trust established)
(3) Working with a remedial teacher is OK.
(4) People can get frustrated yet continue to engage.
(5) He can excel.

The teacher identified:

(1) Processing style (spatial, linguistic, motor, memory) and frustration tolerance;
(2) Response to positive feedback (behavior modification, extrinsic motivators);
(3) Genuine interest in doing well;
(4) Strong academic potential;
(5) Willingness to engage; and
(6) Rapid learning curve.

Session Two

Assessment: This session's goal was to determine the child's current academic standing. High-interest tasks were presented. The results confirmed an
ability to recite the alphabet and name its letters. Also noted, most grapheme
(letter) to phoneme (sound) relationships were established (still missing were
the sounds for all short vowels and the consonants *w, y, x, q*). Concepts of
Print were fair, and both sound blending and sound discrimination seemed
adequate. In contrast, auditory closure and sequential memory were identified
areas of concern.

Treatment: Assessment tasks were game-like. A scorecard (competition as
motivation) was kept. This provided the opportunity "to read who was win-
ning" (experience chart). The "games" ended with mutual signatures confirming, "I agree." A "Note to Mom" reporting the session's outcome was
produced (teacher dictated and scribed).

Note to Mom
I did not win—signed "I agree" (Teacher)
I did win—signed "I agree" (Student)

Impact: The child "proofreads" to confirm the content is accurate. Oral reading begins!

Session Three

This session introduces remedial tasks. Missing consonant and vowel sounds
were taught via mnemonics. Instruction began with discussion (concept) and
modeling (content) of the cuing systems (*Reading in a Nutshell* strategies: The
Known Grapheme > The Unknown Phoneme). Sound associations were practiced and applied in a high-interest game-like format. As before, scores were kept.

The teacher expresses concern about sending home another "I did not
win" note to Mom. The child is delighted! The "games" end, and scores are
tabulated. This child is strong in math, so he totals the result (emphasizing
areas of strength). Now, a more elaborate "Note to Mom" is teacher dictated,
scribed, and read:

Dear Mom,
I got 7 right. Ms. Nickie got 2 right. I won. I got more. I am proud.

The instructor comments, "OK, I think I said the correct thing. I have to
check because sometimes I make mistakes (defusing the negative impact of
miscues). But that's OK because checking helps me learn. It is what smart
people like you and me do" (modeling grit).

Again, I orally read the note. (At this point, the student has had several opportunities to hear its content.) "Yes, that sounds right, but you check to be sure. I don't want to give your mom the wrong information." The student chorally "reads" the "note" (experience chart) to confirm content. Both parties sign, "I agree."

The session ends. The child takes the "Note" to bring home to Mom. Returning to his class, I comment, "Read your note to Mom to let her know you did very good work today. Tell her that I said you should get a prize (a reward plan had been previously arranged with the parent: Extrinsic Motivator). Tell her I am proud of you" (Intrinsic Motivator).

At this point, the treatment plan has presented:

(1) Letter-sound practice through game-like activities
(2) Experience charts for oral reading
(3) Modeled frustration tolerance
(4) Extrinsic and intrinsic motivators
(5) Fail-proof instruction (Safety)
(6) Student-validated success ("I agree")
(7) Incorporated areas of strength (Math Computation)
(8) Format consistency

Session Four

Motivation

The student is met with the query, "Are you planning to win again today? I hope I can finally win!" The youngster walks into the session eager to engage.

Review

"Games" begin. Letter cards (with and without visual clues) are presented to practice the recently established phoneme associations. The teacher notes, "You win again!" and adds, "I feel frustrated, but that's ok because I will not give up!" (For this child, poor frustration tolerance was a marked presenting problem; modeling the need to defuse this concern and to build "power" over it was an important part of his treatment plan.)

New Task

A book is introduced. As soon as presented, the child rejects it, crying out, "I can't read." This emotional reactivity is quickly defused. "That's OK, I will read it for you." As the pages are turned, the student realizes the high-interest story contains only pictures, no text (Safety). He begins to engage, comfortably "reading" along.

New Concept

"Reading is knowing what the story is about. You knew what it was about, so you were reading. It's like when people say you're reading their mind." To demonstrate this concept (contextual analysis), a game is introduced where the child "reads" the teacher's mind. Choosing from a deck of picture cards, I describe an image: "It's a pet. He has fur. He is not a cat. He can bark. He is a__." The child "guesses" and accuracy is confirmed (the revealed picture of a dog). Comment, "See, you read my mind. And reading a book is like that too. The author gives you clues so you can tell what he is thinking about. Your job is to just figure it out!"

Application

The teacher orally reads a simple sentence strip while covering the last word. "I like to eat sandwiches made with peanut butter and __." The student provides a missing word ("jelly"). The teacher comments, "That sounds possible, let's prove it." By tracking the letters of the "guessed word," accuracy is confirmed (and a new strategy, "Prove it," is introduced).

Closure

As before (consistency), a "Note to Mom" (word count increased) is written, mutually confirmed (orally read by teacher and then child), and signed in agreement. The "Note" provides Sight Vocabulary review and practice. Also, it promotes a positive parent-child interaction. Once a provocative task, reading at home has become an opportunity for praise (Intrinsic Motivator) and reward (Extrinsic Motivator).

Sessions Five through Ten

Decoding and encoding instruction continue through games and high-interest activities. Success is guaranteed and praised! More complex experience charts (Academic Component) are presented, practiced, and reviewed. New strategies are applied (phonetic decoding, contextual "guessing," self-monitoring, "Prove it!"). Metacognition, frustration tolerance, and grit develop.

Rapport builds because "safety" is ensured. Academic tasks incorporate the learner's good intellectual potential. Student concerns and frustration are recognized, discussed, and defused.

Instructional Scope and Sequence

(1)   Symbol-Sound Association: Vowels, Consonants, Blends
(2)   Oral Reading: "Note to Mom" (Sight Vocabulary)
(3)   Choral Reading: Rebus Books

(4) Independent Reading: "Wordless" Books (Safety)

(5) Contextual Analysis: Omitted-word "guesses" (Cloze Technique)

(6) Self-monitoring: "Prove it" Strategies

(7) Visual Discrimination: Michigan Tracking and Same-Different Word Pairs

(8) Decoding and Encoding: cvc patterns

(9) Prediction: Picture-clue sentence strips (anticipating content and vocabulary)

(10) Linguistic Decoding: Two-syllable words (trigram + trigram)

(11) Affective Development: Defused Perfectionism, Grit (modeled and praised)

Impact

Leaving the tenth session, the child states, "By the way, I always knew how to read." This comment underscores the student's previously unfulfilled desire to succeed and implies that he now sees himself as competent. The door to literacy has been opened.

Chapter 18

Informal Assessment

Working with students will continuously reveal areas of strength and of concern. Still, a mini diagnostic screening can provide a useful starting point. Short-lived (forty-five to sixty minutes) and well-honed (randomly selected items from standard psychoeducational protocols), the results suggest perceptual style (Visual, Auditory, and Integrative Processing), on-task behavior (Attention), linguistic ability (Receptive and Expressive Language Processing), and affective needs (motivation, frustration tolerance). *The goal is not to obtain scores, percentile ranks, or grade equivalents but rather to identify a student's most overt interferences to learning, that is, what is happening and, most importantly, why.*

Method: Present several random items (five or six) from common diagnostic protocols. If the student moves along without error, discontinue task. (Ongoing remedial lessons will confirm, rule out, or fine-tune the initial impression.)

Materials: The following protocols and items are suggested to establish a working baseline:

(1) Visual Skills

   (a) Slingerland Visual Discrimination and Visual Memory Subtests

   Error patterns suggest difficulty with attending to or recalling the salient characteristics in letters and words (Sequence, Spatial Orientation).

   (b) Detroit Visual Absurdities Subtest

   Error patterns imply a weakness in noting or interpreting visual information.

(c)   Colored overlays

Enhanced Visual Attention (ruling out photosensitivity).

(2)   Auditory Skills

(a)   Sound Discrimination

The Wepman Test of Auditory Discrimination is well regarded and frequently used to assess this skill. To begin, position the student so that he cannot view the evaluator's mouth. Next, orally present word pairs. The child will determine if the items are "the same" or "not the same." (The Wepman manual seeks the response "same" or "different." But, particularly for younger children, the term "different" sometimes causes confusion.)

Note: Be sure to include short e-i pairs (pin/pen) and th-v pairs (clove/clothe). These combinations are often most telling.

(b)   Blending

The Roswell-Chall Auditory Blending Test is a useful protocol. Orally present a word in isolated segments (c-a-t-ch). The student merges the phonemes to identify it ("catch"). Administering a few items should rule out a potential weakness.

(c)   Closure

Some students can discriminate sounds and blend them yet still have difficulty with auditory closure, that is, the ability to identify a word if some sound components are omitted (ele-ant). Among others, Roswell-Chall offers an Auditory Closure Test. Again, only a few items need to be administered should the student fare well.

(d)   Sound Location and Sequencing

The LAC Test (Lindamood) confirms phoneme identification within a word. If a student overtly struggles with this auditory task and acuity is not a factor, referral to rule out a central auditory processing deficit is suggested. An audiologist determines diagnosis.

(e)   Rhyming

Orally present a Traditional List, and ask the student to "add a word." If unsuccessful, present a Concept Enhanced List. (This format better clarifies the nature of the task.) Student response will confirm or rule out a suspected weakness.

Traditional List	Concept Enhancing List
hat, cat, sat, mat	hamburger, shmamburger, waberger
bell, tell, well, fell	telephone, bellephone, zelephone
see, we, me, he	spaghetti, confetti, lometti, bisgetti
all, ball, call, mall	elephant, telephant, welephant, melephant

(3) Fine-Motor Skills

    (a) Spatial Concepts

Handwriting instruction (manuscript and cursive) can be confusing to students who do not understand directional words or spatial concepts ("Start *on* the line, move *up*, curve to the *right*, trace back to the *bottom*, extend the *curve*. That's the letter C").

Task: Have the student engage in a simple origami project to assess spatial knowledge and word meaning (left, right, center, edge).

    (b) Visual-Motor Integration

The Beery-Buktenica Test (VMI) is an easy protocol to administer. Student performance indicates an ability to analyze and reproduce visual information. This copying task also provides an opportunity to observe frustration tolerance and "grit."

Impressions: Note the angle of the student's head/body/tripod to the paper. Also, observe the motor sequence used to reproduce a given form. (Was the design drawn as a gestalt or a series of detail? From the top-down or the bottom-up?) Finally, note effective use of space. (Was the reproduction too large or small, centered or placed to the side?)

    (c) Harris Test of Dominance

This is a quick and fun task that suggests hand, foot, and eye dominance. It also helps break up the testing process by providing an opportunity for the student to stand up and move around.

    (d) Handwriting

Slingerland Copying Tasks are telling. Note performance as well as accuracy. Be aware of the motor sequence used to form letters, their placement on a line, the distance (white space) within and between copied words, and the student's pencil grip. Also, note any mouth, lip, or tongue movements (motor overlay) and how frequently the student referred back to the stimulus (visual recall).

(4) Reading Readiness

    (a) Concepts of Print

        Younger students: Provide a visually clear, grade-appropriate book, and ask the child to show where the story begins and where it ends. Also, determine if he can locate a letter, word, sentence, capital, period, question mark, paragraph, chapter, and title.

        Older students: Using a classroom textbook, confirm the above, and note the student's ability to identify the table of contents, glossary, index, and any supportive visual clues (italics, bolding, charts, and images). Query the purpose for each.

    (b) Alphabet Skills

        Have the student recite the alphabet, match uppercase to lowercase forms, name uppercase and lowercase letters, give the sound for uppercase and lowercase letters, write dictated uppercase and lowercase letters, and name the letter for a given sound.

(5) Word Recognition

    (a) Sight Vocabulary

        (1) A Dolch List or Frye List can be used to screen basic words.

        (2) Higher-level graded word lists are found in most standard reading test protocols (e.g., the Woodcock Reading Mastery Test or the Wide Range Achievement Test).

    (b) Decoding

        (1) Confirm letter-to-sound associations are established.

        (2) Determine mastery of basic syllable patterns (vc, cV, cvc, cVce, cVvc).

        (3) Confirm sound associations for blends, digraphs, diphthongs, R-controlled vowels, prefixes, and suffixes.

    (c) Contextual Analysis

        (1) Provide the opportunity to "Read My Mind" through oral language game-like tasks.

        (2) Cloze passages (paragraphs with space holders for deleted words) are also useful.

(6) Language Processing

    (a) Assess informal conversation. (If the child seems confused by oral directions or reticent to engage in discussion, referral for a speech-language evaluation may be warranted.)

    (b) To determine effective syntactic processing, present basic sentence pairs like *The boy dropped peas in the soup* versus *The boy dropped soup in the peas*. Ask, "What's different?"

    (c) Use idioms and multiple-meaning words to imply semantic mastery.

In summary, know your student! Note which hand he uses to hold a pencil; the number of items he can complete; any correlations between speed and accuracy; the sentence structure, articulation, and vocabulary he uses; his affect in response to task difficulty; his willingness to engage; and his level of frustration tolerance. Most important, be aware that queries like "What were you thinking when you did that?" can prove more telling than any standardized test results.

Appendix

I. OVERALL SCHEMA

The Science	The Art
Letter-Sound Relationships	Minimized Memory Load
Basic Decoding	Accurate Auditory and Visual Processing
Linguistic Decoding	Ensured Sound Association
Miscue Analysis	Defused "Error Power"
Academic Support	Affective Support

II. SCOPE AND SEQUENCE CHART

Useful to confirm that reading tasks are finite. This chart can also provide a source for comparing initial to current standing (a benchmark for progress made).

EVERYTHING THAT A GOOD READER NEEDS TO KNOW

(1) Associate graphemes to phonemes
(2) Recognize and spell sight vocabulary words ("Modified List")
(3) "Read minds" (Contextual Analysis)
(4) Analyze multisyllable words (Linguistic Decoding, Block Arrays)
(5) Self-talk (Consider optional strategies)
(6) Active reading (Conversation with the Author)

III. SIGHT VOCABULARY

Sight vocabulary refers to basic words that require immediate recognition. Both the Dolch and Frye lists present these "instant words."

(A) The Standard List (A Primary Source for Spelling Practice)

Pre-K Dolch Sight Words:

a, and, big, can, come, for, go, help, here, I, in, is, it, jump, little, look, make, me, my, not, one, play, red, run, see, the, to, up, we, you

Kindergarten Dolch Sight Words:

all, am, are, at, ate, be, black, brown, but, came, did, do, eat, four, get, good, have, he, help, into, like, must, new, no, now, on, our, out, please, pretty, ran, ride, said, saw, say, she, so, soon, that, there, they, this, too, two, under, want, was, well, went, what, white, who, will, with, yes

First-Grade Dolch Sight Words:

after, again, an, any, as, ask, by, could, every, fly, from, give, going, had, has, her, him, his, how, just, know, let, live, may, of, old, once, open, over, put, round, some, stop, take, thank, them, then, think, walk, were, when, where, yellow, your

Second-Grade Dolch Sight Words:

always, around, because, been, before, best, both, buy, call, cold, does, don't, fast, first, five, found, gave, goes, green, its, made, many, off, or, pull, read, right, sing, sit, sleep, tell, their, these, those, upon, us, use, very, wash, which, why, wish, work, would, write

Third-Grade Dolch Sight Words:

about, better, bring, carry, clean, cut, done, draw, drink, eight, fall, far, full, got, grow, hold, hot, hurt, if, keep, kind, laugh, light, long, much, myself, never, only, own, pick, seven, shall, show, six, small, start, ten, today, together, try, warm

Noun Dolch Sight Words:

apple, baby, back, ball, bear, bed, bell, bird, birthday, boat, box, boy, bread, brother, cake, car, cat, chair, chicken, children, coat, corn, cow, day, dog, doll, door, duck, egg, eye, farm, farmer, father, feet, fire, fish, floor, flower, game, garden, girl, goodbye, grass, ground, hand, head, hill, home, horse, house, kitty, leg, letter, man, men, milk, money, morning, mother, name, nest, night, paper, party, picture, pig, rabbit, rain, ring, robin, school, seed, sheep, shoe, sister, snow, song, squirrel, stick, street, sun, table, thing, time, top, toy, tree, watch, water, way, wind, window, wood

(B) A Simplified List

The majority of Dolch words are phonetically regular. The following is a modified version of the standard list. It contains only those high-frequency words that cannot be easily decoded.

Modified List

is	of	the	to	look	more	off
by	other	right	some	two	want	were
their	only	what	where	who	your	was
come	off	more	look	into	here	been
are	before	have	from	do	could	call
one	said	they	you			

(C) Visual "Wholes"

Like Sight Vocabulary, these word parts require immediate recognition:

(1) Diphthongs

aw   au   ew   oo   ou   ow

(2) Digraphs

th   wh   sh   kn   wr   ph

(3) R-Controlled Vowels

er,   ar,   ir,   or,   ur

(4) Suffixes

-able   -al   -ful   -ial   -ic   -ing   -tion

-ity   -ative,   -itive   -less   -ly   -ture

(5) Prefixes

auto-   anti-   bi-   fore-   tri-   octo-   semi-   uni-

(6) Sound Clusters

all   ay   igh   ind   ang   ank   ink   ough

IV. WORD KNOWLEDGE

(A) Transition Words

These higher-level words and phrases should be recognized not only as sight vocabulary but also for the purpose they serve. Mastery enhances reading comprehension and written expression.

Addition: And, in addition, furthermore, moreover, besides, also, another, next, likewise, for example, for instance, thus, therefore.

Concession: Although, at least, still, even though, granted that, while it may be true, in spite of, of course.

Consequence or Result: Thus, for this reason, therefore, so, because, since, due to, as a result, in other words.

Contrast: But, however, nevertheless, in spite of, in contrast, yet, or, nor, conversely.

Examples: For example, for instance, to illustrate, thus, in other words, in particular, namely.

Summary: Therefore, finally, in short, in conclusion.

Time: After, afterward, before, then, next, finally, soon, meanwhile, later, previously, in the meantime, immediately, eventually, simultaneously.

(B) Frequently Confused Words

accept (agree) – except (not part of)   affect (feeling) – effect (result)

all ready (complete) – already (by now)   angel (spirit) – angle (arithmetic term)

desert (arid land) – dessert (food)   envelop (surround) – envelope (paper cover)

human (person) – humane (kind hearted)   lay (put down) – lie (recline)

loose (not tight) – lose (misplace)   pasture (field) – Pastor (religious leader)

picture (illustration) – pitcher (container)   precede (before) – proceed (go on)

quiet (still) – quite (very)   than (compared to) – then (when)

(C) Common Homophones

celler-seller   flour-flower

bored-board   hire-higher

aloud-allowed   principal-principle

chews-choose   whether-weather

V. CUBE ARRAY PRACTICE WORDS

(A) The CVC Pattern (blue + white + blue)

men	can	hit	nut
tin	him	did	not
top	fish	flat	lick
ship	chop	has	with
thumb	last	shop	strap
clog	step	trip	brag
fast	rest	jump	stack

(B) The CVC/CVC Pattern (blue + white + blue/blue + white + blue)

rabbit	bottom	attach
hammock	traffic	kitten
lesson	sudden	blanket
pilgrim	happen	pumpkin
complex	himself	sunset
suspend	solvent	problem

(C) The CV/CVC Pattern (blue + white/blue + white + blue)

focus	music	pilot
humid	human	defend
silent	humor	frozen

(D) The CVCe "Stacked" Pattern (blue + "tower" + blue)

mode	spade	home
save	tone	game
tape	pole	crate
dine	clove	trade

(E) The CVvC "Stacked" Pattern (blue +"tower"+blue)

meal	weak	seat
teach	streak	clean
beat	reach	dream
reap	beast	stream
yeast	strain	throat

(F) The PREFIX Pattern (yellow + block array)

exit	extend	express
incorrect	indent	include

nonfat	forecast	foremost
tripod	trigram	octopus
unwrap	refill	retake

(G) The SUFFIX Pattern (block array + yellow)

finish	restless	hopeless
weakness	painful	illness
misty	lastly	loudly
faster	lesser	coolest
homeless	fewest	dimly

(H) The -LE Pattern (block array + "white dot" cubes)

castle	wrestle	whistle
pickle	buckle	circle
gentle	chuckle	table

(I) DIPHTHONGS and R-CONTROLLED Patterns ("white dot" cubes)

moon	lampoon	harpoon
frown	prowl	ouch
maul	launch	August
oyster	convoy	destroy
thirty	story	orbit
form	term	hermit
confirm	birth	skirmish

(J) COMPLEX WORDS (multiple patterns)

| archaic | admonish | dissolution |
| orthodox | didactic | disconcerting |

VI. LITERATURE RESOURCES

(A) High Interest-Low Readability Books

High Interest-Low Reading Level Books for Reluctant Readers
www.thoughtco.com/books-for-reluctant-readers-627603

Far-Fetched News: Fables and Folktales Presented as Front Page News Articles
December 19, 2008, by Sherrill B. Flora M.S.

High Interest/Low Reading Level Book List
www.schoolonwheels.org/pdfs/3328/Hi-Lo-Book-List.pdf

High Interest/Low Reading Level Books
www.sdlback.com/hi-lo-reading

High Interest Low Readability Books for Struggling Readers
thisreadingmama.com/high-interest-low-readability-books

Where To Find High Interest, Low Level Reading Books (Hi/Lo Readers).
Blog. www.friendshipcircle.org/blog/2012/12/20/where-to-find-high

HIP Books for Reluctant & Struggling Readers
hip-books.com

Popular High Interest Low Level Books—Goodreads
www.goodreads.com/shelf/show/high-interest-low-level

(B) "Wordless" Books (Text-Free Literature)

Raines, S. C., and Isbell, R. (1988). Tuck talking about wordless books in your class. *Young Children, 43*(6), 24–25.
Richey, V. H., and Puckett, K. E. (1992). *Wordless/almost wordless picture books: A guide*. Englewood, CO: Libraries Unlimited.

(C) Graphic Novels Reading Lists (ALA.org)

Annually updated, the American Library Association list (Gr. K–8).

(D) Books on Tape (Literature and Academic Textbooks)

Free Public Library Service is available for Dyslexic students.

VII. PARENT RESOURCES

Dyslexia Advocate! How to Advocate for a Child with Dyslexia within the Public Education System by Kelli Sandman-Hurley (Author)

Parent Guide to Special Education
www2.ed.gov

International Dyslexia Association
dyslexiaida.org

LD Online
ldonline.org

Learning Disability Association of America
idaamerica.org

National Center for Learning Disabilities
ncld.org

Understood
understood.org

VIII. STUDENT RESOURCES

Learning Outside the Lines by Jonathan Mooney, David Cole
goodreads.com

*Keeping a Head in School: A Student's Book about Learning Abilities and
   Learning Disorders* by Melvin D. Levine (Author)
amazon.com

School Smarts by Jay Amberg
www.amazon.com/School-Smarts-Jay-Amberg/dp/0673361365

Ticonderoga Tri-Write Pencil
Triangular pencils. This shape is comfortable to hold and supports proper
   pencil grip.

Free Dyslexia Fonts
www.free-fonts.com/dyslexia
High-quality fonts considered helpful by children and adults with Dyslexia.

Photo-math: Free Download
appreviewed.net/photomath

You Tube: Homework Helpers
Kohn Academy Instructional Videos (Science, Mathematics, Literature)

The Classics: High-Interest Video

Hip-hop music summaries (*Hamlet, Huck Finn, The Scarlet Letter*, etc.)
www.flocabulary.com/topics/literature

Thug Notes
www.wisecrack.co/thug-notes

References

THE VALUABLE "KERNELS OF TRUTH."

Authors

Chall, J. S. (1967). *Learning to read: The great debate.* Fort Worth, TX: Harcourt Brace College Publishers.

Freire, Paulo. (1968). *Pedagogy of the oppressed.* Translated by Myra B. Ramos. www.goodreads.com/book/show/72657.

Harnadek, Anita. (2008). *Math word problems: Book 1.* Seaside, CA: The Critical Thinking Co. (CriticalThinking.com).

Lavoie, Richard. (1989). *How difficult can this be? The F.A.T. city workshop.* www.ricklavoie.com.

Maslow, Abraham. (1943). *Maslow hierarchy of needs.* www.abraham-maslow.com/m_motivation/Hierarchy_of_Needs.asp.

Ramus, F., Altarelli, I., Jednoróg, K., Zhao, J., and Scotto di Covella, L. (2018). Neuroanatomy of developmental dyslexia: Pitfalls and promise. *Neuroscience & Biobehavioral Reviews, 84,* 434–452.

Scarborough, H. S. (2005). Developmental relationships between language and reading. *Journal of Speech and Hearing Research, 33,* 70–83.

Sheehy, Gail. (1974). *Passages: Predictable crises of adult life.* New York: Ballantine Books. https://books.google.com/books/about/Passages.html?id=rY3dWN88Q7UC.

Simpson, Eileen. (1991). *Reversals: A personal account of victory over dyslexia.* Boston: Houghton Mifflin. Amazon.com.

Resources

Cognitive Behavioral Therapy (CBT): Self-Talk. www.prohealth.com/library/show-article.cfm?libid=12800.

Dolch Sight Word Stories—readinghawk.com. www.readinghawk.com/Reading_ Hawk/Dolch_Sight_Word_Stories.html.

Dolch Word List—Dolch Sight Words. www.dolchsightwords.org/dolch_word_ list.php.

Glass Analysis info Is Easier to Learn, Inc. (1970). Garden City, NY.

Irlen Vision Testing. www.irlenvisions.com/pg/Testing-for-Irlen-Syndrome.php.

Lindamood Auditory Conceptualization Test—Third Edition. http://ganderpublishing. com/product/lindamood-auditory-conceptualization-test.asp.

Lindamood-Bell Auditory In Depth Program. ganderpublishing.com/content/ welcome-to-lindamood-bell.asp.

Lindamood Phoneme Sequencing Program (LiPS). www.lblp.com.

Reading Recovery Program—Reading Recovery. readingrecovery.education.gsu.edu/ reading-recovery-program.

Recipe for reading by Nina Traub (1977, Hardcover) | eBay. https://www.ebay. com/p/Recipe-for-Reading-by-Nina-Traub-1977-Hardcover/1614453? iid=302442335506.

Using Image Analysis to Build Reading Comprehension. files.eric.ed.gov/fulltext/ EJ916613.pdf.

Visual tracking (1969 edition) | Open Library (Michigan Tracking Program). https:// openlibrary.org/books/OL18392757M/Visual_tracking?v=1.

The reading teacher's book of lists, 6th edition. Wiley. www.wiley.com/WileyCDA/ WileyTitle/productCd-111908105X.html.

Postscript

1975 Public Law (P.L. 94–142) requires Special Education Services for Dyslexic Students.

1987 Public School Special Education Meeting for a Dyslexic Lower-School Student.

(1)   Initial Recommendation: "Provide a Classroom Computer."
(2)   Parent Follow-Up: "Provide a Classroom Computer *That Works.*"
(3)   Advocate Follow-Up: "Provide a Classroom Computer That Works *with a Nearby Outlet so It Can Be Plugged In.*"

2017 Public School Special Education Meeting for a Dyslexic High School Student.

(1)   Initial Recommendation: "Provide a Computer-Based Reading Program."
(2)   Advocate Follow-Up: "Provide a Computer-Based Reading Program *That Develops Decoding Skills.*"

A Dyslexic student's instructional plan requires ongoing monitoring. Well-intended IEP (Individual Education Plan) and RTI (Response to Intervention) supports may fail to translate in the regular classroom setting. The aforementioned examples of follow-up modifications to an original IEP reflect the efforts of vigilant parents, teachers, and child advocates. Were the initial inadequacies not brought to the attention of the Public School, an ineffective plan would have remained in place.

Remember, Dyslexia is an invisible handicap. As such, bright struggling students often become the victims of their own disability, misperceived as "crazy, lazy, or stupid." Such logic often justifies their limited academic gains. *Know that stagnant progress in bright children with reading disabilities is unacceptable.* It indicates that something is awry.

About the Author

Nickie Simonetti holds graduate degrees in the teaching of reading and has served as a classroom teacher, resource teacher, reading specialist, educational evaluator, teacher-training consultant, parent advocate, special education program director, and adjunct professor.

Over the years, though titles became grander, none surpassed "teacher." Of that, she is most proud.